COMMON-SENSE SUICIDE

Doris Portwood

COMMON SENSE SUICIDE

The Final Right

The Hemlock Society
Los Angeles
Distributed by Grove Press
New York

The Hemlock Society acknowledges
with gratitude the gracious gift
of the copyright of this book
by Doris Portwood.

Library of Congress Cataloging in Publication Data

Portwood, Doris,
  Common-sense suicide.

  1. Suicide. 2. Aged. I. Title.

HV6$_{545}$.P66 $_3$6$_4$.I'522 $_7$8$_{-959}$

ISBN: 0-394-62013-5

Published by the Hemlock Society,
P.O. Box 66218, Los Angeles,
California 90066

Distributed by Grove Press Inc.
196 West Houston St., New York
NY 10014

CONTENTS

INTRODUCTION

OLDER women have so far made only a small contribution to the women's movement. Our role is largely passive; we discover the convenience of pants suits and insulate our ears against the shock of four-letter words. We bring a gift of tolerance for the life styles and language of a liberated generation. We accept and adapt—even sometimes approve. But we do not crusade.

This is unfortunate, because senior American women have a unique opportunity to promote a long overdue social reform. We have seen most taboos disappear in recent years. Our granddaughters may choose (or refuse) to live in an openly unmarried state with young men. They may apply for jobs previously denied to women—and may sue if they fail to get them. They may openly support abortion, or openly oppose it. Mass demonstrations now back the rights of homosexual minorities (female or male) who guarded their identity with fearful care only a generation ago. Censorship of books

9

and films has become minimal. Almost no subject is barred from full discussion on TV talk shows or in the media.

Almost none.

An exception is rational suicide for the older person. It needs to be talked about and American women of social security age are the ones to start the talking. There are so many of us—close to 15 million over-65 women and 145 for every 100 men in the same age group. And we live so long—outdistancing men by more than eight years.

Senior American women have wealth and power. Yet hundreds of thousands end their lives in baffled misery in the near imprisonment of nursing home or hospital. Others are alone, clinging to a familiar place when it no longer provides the needed comforts. Still others, living with a relative, feel the disruption of their own lives and suffer guilt for the disruption they know their presence imposes.

Few would choose any of the common fates of the ailing elderly. How many of us, attending a friend or relative in her final days (or weeks, or months, or years) have said, "It won't happen to me. I'll take care of that."

But did we say it aloud?

It is time to say it loud and clear. And often. We can borrow a phrase from the new vocabulary and declare our intention to start a meaningful dialogue 10 on common-sense suicide.

1

IT'S TIME TO TALK
ABOUT SUICIDE

IN 46 B.C., Cato the Younger, facing military defeat and after evacuating his troops, decided on suicide. He secluded himself in his quarters, read passages from Plato's *Phaedo,* and stabbed himself. He lost consciousness but did not die. Recovering consciousness, he found his wounds bound up and physicians attending him. He physically rejected the physicians' ministrations, tore off his bandages and died. Seneca, extolling Cato's death, said, "Jupiter himself could not have seen anything more beautiful on earth."

In the early Christian era the devout maiden Blandina courted martyrdom by offering herself for torture when (according to her chronicler) "a day of fighting with beasts was specially appointed for the Christians" who defied Roman edicts against their faith. Surviving the day's event, she "went rejoicing" to yet another contest where, finally, having been "put in a net and thrown to a bull," she achieved her aim and became a sacrifice.

In England in the 1860s, a man who had cut his throat was arrested for the crime and condemned to die by hanging. A doctor pointed out that such a procedure would open the slit throat, admit air—and foil the noose. But the hanging went on regardless, with the authorities determined to do their duty toward the sinning would-be suicide. His throat did open, as predicted, but he was bandaged and patched up sufficiently to keep life within him just long enough for it to be snuffed out by the prescribed punishment.

In the 1970s, an elderly couple living in one of New York's better nursing homes tried to commit double suicide by slashing each other. They did not have very suitable implements in their room; probably they were also weak. Before undertaking the task they had left a brief note, which was found when the sounds of the effort attracted attention and they were interrupted. They were hospitalized—presumably to recover and begin again the long wait for release.

All these incidents are brutal. In each case they show a different attitude to the fact of suicide. Surely the last example, in our age of enlightenment, is the least understandable. Circumstances should not come to this in the late twentieth century. Suicide need not be raised to the heroic stature it enjoyed under the Romans, nor embraced with the frantic delight of the primitive Christians. But neither must it continue to be seen as the sin, the crime and the shame that are equally distorted views.

It is time to talk about all these things.

Even the vocabulary of suicide has been affected by the taboo. The wide use of "attempted suicide" by police and medical authorities has made an opposite term necessary—yet there is obvious distaste for "successful suicide." The language purist may argue that there cannot be "successful" suicide because suicide itself means the achieved act (i.e., built-in success). If one takes this view, there also cannot be "attempted suicide," but the public records are already too full of the term, and it is too obviously useful and well-understood to be discarded at this point. Some writers and commentators use "completed" as an alternative to "successful," but this term has not gained popular usage.

Other writers on the subject of suicide have suggested that we need a different vocabulary. Self-termination or self-determination are suggested, also self-destruction. The former terms call up scenes of U.N. debate rather than a personal situation, while the final one reminds us, ruefully perhaps, that the human body does not self-destruct in this age of mechanical miracles and throwaway packaging.

Suicide is a good word. We all know what it means and we have no valid reason to avoid it. It is   13 a relatively new word for an old institution. The word seems to have been coined from a Latin base in the mid-1600s. It did not gain common usage and did not appear even in Dr. Johnson's 1755 *Dictionary*. The *Oxford English Dictionary* says the term first was used in 1651 when Walter Charleton said, "To vindicate one's self from inevitable Calamity, by Suicide is not . . . a crime."

Shakespeare, lacking the word, was at no loss to use the act of suicide generously in his dramas. In the "to be or not to be" soliloquy it is "self-slaughter"; in many of his references a phrase or line is required to convey the thought. Juliet, beside Romeo's body, says, "Poison, I see, hath been his timeless end." And Juliet herself, using Romeo's dagger, speaks to it: "O happy dagger! This is thy sheath; there rest, and let me die."

The Bible, which reports a number of suicides without a word of condemnation, simply describes the circumstances. Saul "fell upon his sword" and Achitophel "put his Household in order and hanged himself." John Donne, English Renaissance poet who wrote the first English-language defense of (or apologia for) suicide, *Biathanatos,* used the term self-homicide. And Sir Thomas Browne wrote (most comfortingly) in his *Religio Medici* in 1642, "We are in the power of no calamity while death is in our own."

14   Fortunately we have a clear and not unpleasing

word to use in our expanded dialogue. Suicide, simply as a word, is in no way objectionable. It is pronounceable, understandable, and specific. It is an adequate term. And it is particularly appropriate to this writing because the dictionary definition accents an age of responsibility. Suicide is (under 1.a. in *Webster's Collegiate*) "the act or an instance of taking one's own life voluntarily and intentionally esp. by a person of years of discretion and of sound mind." That is what we're talking about.

Some of the most open discussion about a right to suicide has come out of San Francisco. This is not surprising because San Francisco has one of the highest suicide rates in the U.S. and also one of the most spectacular suicide sites—the Golden Gate Bridge. Controversy about suicides from this bridge sparked a lively debate about the time the 500th suicide was expected in the fall of 1973. (The 600 mark was passed in 1977.) The public and media awaited No. 500 with a heightened interest that authorities felt might have the adverse effect of hastening a decision by potential suicides. The bridge staff were on the alert to try to stave off the inevitable for as long as possible. The manager of the Golden Gate Bridge District outlined for concerned civic leaders and the press the measures that were in force to prevent suicides. These included a 24-hour motorized patrol, indoctrination of the bridge staff (including painters) by the FBI on what to watch for in personality traits, the closing of all walkways at night and installation of closed-circuit television cameras that could see through the darkness to spot anyone who left a car and tried to go over the rail. Fourteen attempts were foiled between No. 499 and the eventual No. 500.

A million-dollar "suicide fence" for the bridge was under consideration at the time and the public attitude, as reflected in mail to the Bridge District, was 75% against the fence. It would be ugly and would mar the grace of the bridge, some said. Many believed it would force people to find other and possibly less suitable means of taking their lives. Those who championed individual civil liberties believed that the bridge should be available for suicides as well as for any other bridge users. One of the local personalities who spoke out was Kurt Adler, director of the opera, who said, "It is everyone's privilege to decide if he wants to live or not. It is not for society to decide that."

While the argument continued, the company that was to undertake a feasibility study for the fence began to have second thoughts. Company executives had been advised by their attorneys that the firm might risk legal liability if some suicides foiled the fence.

During the ongoing discussions, No. 500, followed in less than 24 hours by No. 501 (one man and one woman), asserted their civil liberties and

16

used the bridge for suicide.

One of the pro-fence opinions at the time was based on the research that had been carried on for some years by Dr. Richard Seiden, a psychologist at the University of California's School of Public Health at Berkeley. His study showed that out of 1440 persons who had been prevented from jumping to their death from the bridge only 4% went on to commit suicide by other means. These figures provided a valid back-up for his opinion that the bridge exerted a kind of fascination that lured to their deaths many who otherwise would overcome their depression and survive.

Need we say that most of these saved-from-suicide persons were young people? There is a continuing increase in suicide by the under-24 age group and few would argue against the need for suicide prevention centers, counselor hot-lines and research projects. When you are under 24, there is so much time to change your mind. People with many productive years to live should be helped to have that chance.

Equally, older persons should be accorded the courtesy of an assumption that we know what we want. By the time we reach 65 most of us have made many decisions. On a private decision we deserve the dignity of a respectful concurrence. When an older woman leaves a social gathering—perhaps an hour after dinner and when younger guests are settling down to a game or a fresh drink—no one urges her to linger on. Someone may call a cab or offer a lift. She will receive thoughtful words during the process of departure, but no insistence on her staying. There is the assumption that she has, in fact, some good reason for going.

When we have a good reason for voluntary departure from life, similar courtesy would be appreciated, but we cannot count on it. On the contrary, we can be quite sure it will *not* be forthcoming. Therefore we must demand it as a right of what has been called the U.S.A.'s fastest-growing minority: the aging.

Within that minority, the majority are women, and both are growing. In the dinner-party example above, the departing woman is alone. This is the way most of us will be situated when we are ready to depart life. No one knows why American women live so long, but the facts of our longevity are well documented. We not only outnumber men 145 to 100 in the 65-plus age group (a ratio that increases to 166 to 100 for 75-and-up) but our habits of marriage, with a younger bride for an older groom, cause additional imbalance. Older men tend to have living wives; most older women are widows. Widows outnumber widowers four to one.

Because of these facts, 80% of older men are living in a family setting and 70% have wives in the household. Older women, on the other hand, live in

18

a family situation in only 61% of cases and have a husband present in only 34%. When disability arrives, most older men have someone to look after them until their statistically more timely departure. Most women do not—which explains the preponderance of women in nursing-home populations.

Our large and growing minority carries increasing weight with politicians. We represent a lot of votes and a big reservoir of human beings who can be counted on to ask for services. We have, too, an exploitable sentimental value or, perhaps more accurately, a guilt value that gives us a chance to be heard. As long as the U.S. observes a multi-billion dollar Mother's Day rite we multitudinous older women will have at least a periodic forum for our opinions. In such forums we can defend old-age suicide as a positive step, a civil right for the new minority, and a common courtesy to the older woman who knows when it is time to go.

2

A SIN, A CRIME AND
A SHAME?

Down through recorded history, suicide
has been many things to many people. To the early
Greeks and Romans it was an honorable way to
avoid capture by an enemy, to avoid the humiliation
of defeat, and to evade death at an enemy's hands.
Suicide was sometimes homage—as in self-destruction by soldiers to honor their fallen chief. Or the
followers of a chieftain might be bound by a vow to
die with their leader.

For the women of the era, suicide at the bier of
their husbands was an honor and privilege. Herodo-
tus wrote of the custom among Thracians (a polyga-
mous society) whereby the wives of the deceased
vied for the honor of being named the most loved.
So named, the honored one was slain over the husband's grave and buried with him. The custom of
suttee among Indian widows, who threw themselves
on the burning pyre of their husbands, was practiced
as long ago as the time of Alexander the Great and

was outlawed only in 1829.

Cleopatra, who chose an unusual death by allowing a poisonous snake to bite her, is the classic example of romantic suicide because of an ill-fated love affair. Her lover Mark Antony had meanwhile killed himself after receiving a then-false report of Cleopatra's death. And the heroic suicide was not limited to men. The wife of a Roman senator who had plotted against the Emperor Claudius gave her husband courage by stabbing herself in the breast and then handing the knife to him, with the comment "It does not hurt."

Greek and Roman philosophers discussed suicide and usually endorsed it within specific limitations. Staunchest of the pro-suicide group were the Stoics, whose founder Zeno is said to have believed that "the wise man will for reasonable cause make his own exit from life on his country's behalf, or for the sake of his friends, or if he suffer intolerable pain, mutilation, or incurable disease."

Most of the suicides of this era were heroic and many were tied to the ups and downs of military conquest. Old-age suicide was not much of a question—life expectancy in ancient Greece is variously reported as being from 23 to 28 years. An exception was Hannibal who, at 74, took the poison he always carried in a ring rather than accede to the Roman demand for his return from voluntary exile. At that time he is said to have remarked that he wanted to spare the Romans the terror an old man inspired in them.

The only association of crime and suicide in Greco-Roman days was in a property sense. Slaves, as commodities, were not allowed to do themselves in, nor were the soldiers whose continued existence was vital to the state.

The early Christians brought a new attitude toward suicide by taking a fanatic delight in the prospect of instant salvation. There was no shortage of candidates for the tortures of the arena: a martyr's death meant a reserved seat among the blessed in heaven. These suicides were, in today's language, passive rather than active. The primitive Christians did not fall on the sword or hold the hemlock cup to their own lips, but they walked willingly—men, women and children—into situations (often deliberately provoked situations) that meant not only death but death of a most grim variety.

The mass suicide of early Christians, however, threatened to decimate the earthly population of the saved by removing them all to the promised afterlife. Reforms were needed, and came in the fourth to sixth centuries A.D. The Council of Braga in 563 specifically condemned suicide (codifying an attitude that had been emerging) and this condemnation was affirmed by later councils. The rationalization for the ban was a broadened interpretation of 22 the commandment "Thou shalt not kill" to include self-destruction. St. Augustine developed the argument that because life is a gift of God, the rejection of life is a rejection of God and God's will—and thus a sin. Because suicide allowed no time for repentance it was extraordinarily sinful.

Although the Augustinian line of reasoning took much from Plato's *Phaedo* (man as a property of the gods) and nothing from the Bible, it persisted as the basic Christian doctrine. Suicide became and continues to be a sin; it was, under a State Church, equally a crime. Its dark side of inexplicit shamefulness seems to have an even earlier origin in the primitive superstitions of a people who lived in dread of the power of ghosts. Suicides were buried at crossroads, sometimes with a stake through the heart, in a practice that continued in England until 1823.

The Vikings brought a touch of variety to the suicide picture by viewing self-destruction as the second path to Valhalla. First place was reserved for those who died in battle. Any who lingered on to die of old age or disease were specifically barred from Valhalla forever.

The Renaissance produced an increase in suicides and a revival of dialogue on the subject. John Donne's *Biathanatos* (subtitled "A Declaration of that Paradoxe, or Thesis, That Self-homicide is not so naturally Sinne, that it may never be otherwise") was the outstanding example of a new look at an old practice, but many other writers, both inside and   23 outside the church, also found the topic useful. Montaigne, in his *Essays,* calls death "a very secure haven, never to be feared and often to be sought." Romantic suicide was used effectively by playwrights and poets. The new permissiveness on the subject allowed the description, without condemnation, of an incident of suicide by the *maitre d'hotel* of the Prince de Condé who took his life in shame when a dinner prepared for Louis XIV did not turn out well.

The discussion led, also, to the surfacing of opposition views and to some early attention to the question of suicide prevention. Two Protestant ministers, in Germany and in England, not only produced sermons on the subject but tried to offer preventive counsel while they continued to study the phenomenon. They both came to the conclusion that people who are so driven by their "vexatious" circumstances that they attempt self-murder are not necessarily damned but mentally deranged. This still is a convenient tag for suicides who might be denied full church rites unless they are deemed not to have been in their right minds at the time of the act.

Although Donne's thesis was written early in the seventeenth century it was not published until 1646, fifteen years after his death. His own view of the work, in his later years, was ambivalent. He recognized it as a "misinterpretable" subject and after he took Anglican orders (he had been born a Catholic) he asked the party to whom he entrusted the manuscript to "publish it not, yet burn it not; and between those, do what you will with it."

Another posthumous publication was David Hume's famous essay "On Suicide," published in 1777, a year after his death. Even then it was immediately suppressed. This essay was then, and remains today, a convincing and quotable argument against the moral prejudice surrounding suicide. Hume argued that if all actions of man were judged in terms of their disturbance of God's design, "it would be equally criminal to act for the preservation of life as for its destruction." He pointed out that man can take few actions that are not *some* kind of interference with God's will—"It would be no crime in me to divert the Nile or Danube from its course, were I able to effect such purposes. Where then is the crime in turning a few ounces of blood from their natural channel?" As for the damage to society, Hume's view was the reasonable one often concurred with by more recent writers that at the worst one does not harm society by suicide but merely ceases to do good (if good works were what one had been up to). He reminds, also, that one who is tired of life often is a burden on society by hindering the usefulness of others.

Modern-day attitudes toward suicide are no less confused and controversial than those of earlier times. The arrival of sociology, psychology and psychiatry cast little light on the dark subject. Emile Durkheim, born in 1858, the French pioneer in the new science of "sociology," wrote his *Le Suicide* in 1897. The study, based on a statistical approach, removed suicide from the moral and criminal context and treated it as a fact of society. The latest papers in medical and mental health journals do roughly the same. They seldom offer anything newer than a more sophisticated way with statistics and sometimes a fresh turn of phrase for a well-worn opinion. The fact that Durkheim's book recently became available in an English-language paperback edition must say something about the progress of suicide research since 1897. Another early work popularly available in paperback is Thomas G. Masaryk's *Suicide and the Meaning of Civilization,* dating from 1881. Newer paperbacks about suicide lean on art film to show the despair and the revival of the rehabilitated attempter, or concentrate on prevention among the alienated young.

Durkheim divided all suicides into three types: egoistic, which is likely to be carried out by the loner, perhaps in a mock-heroic or romantic context; altruistic, in which the group comes first and suicide is sacrifice for a cause or a comrade; the anomic, wherein the individual suffers disorientation, or *anomie,* and cannot make the necessary adjustment to quick-change circumstances.

26   Number three, of course, typifies today's society.

Anomie is the rule rather than the exception. More adjustment is demanded than can be supplied. Future shock meets yesterday's theories and something has to give—often it is the individual's ability to cope. When we are old enough and tired enough, such inability is surely excusable. Can we not ask permission to leave quietly while the experts continue to argue what suicide is all about?

Varying attitudes toward suicide have emerged in the short-run as well as the long. Usually they are sparked by an increase in the suicide rate or by some peculiar circumstance that makes suicide more noticeable if not more frequent. Such a period in our century came in the 1930s, when an inexplicable increase in suicides brought the subject to popular attention. (The number peaked in 1932 with nearly 21,000 suicides in the U.S. at a time when our population was only 125 million; this is in contrast to the 1975 total of less than 27,000 in a population of 215 million.) An assumption that it was a result of the depression was not fully borne out by investigation, although economic conditions probably were responsible for some part of the increase. No satisfactory explanation was found, although in hindsight present day writers on the subject automatically link the record rates of 1932–1933 to the depression.

In any case, the subject was popular and the overall attitude rather light. Jean Bruller, the French writer and illustrator who later was active in the

French underground in World War II and wrote under the pseudonym of Vercors, was young and carefree enough in 1930 to turn out a book called *21 Delightful Ways of Committing Suicide,* complete with color drawings that a *New York Times* review called "grim, jesting, faintly Goyesque." The book was published in the U.S. and sold for $2.00. Dorothy Parker wrote her famous verse ("Razors pain you, rivers are damp . . .") itemizing seven means of escape and their drawbacks.

The 1930s had their complainers from the other side too. A writer in *Atlantic Monthly* deplored the fact that "nowadays it seems to be the vogue to call egoistic those who prefer the idea of some sort of personal survival to that of extinction." But suicide went on, and in those pre-Golden Gate Bridge days another California bridge figured in the news. The Colorado Street bridge over the Arroyo Seco in Pasadena was cited as a place from which all too many "hurled themselves to destruction." The bridge police were considering how to install safety nets on each side of the bridge—no million-dollar fences in the depression years.

A highlight of the 1930s suicide coverage is the death of a famous feminist in 1935. Mrs. Charlotte Perkins Gilman had begun lecturing in 1890 on ethics, economy and sociology. She was named by Carrie Chapman Catt as one of the "twelve greatest American women" and was given primary rank among these because, as Mrs. Catt explained, "there was a period in the women's movement when she brought out first one book and then another. . . . And I credit those books with utterly revolutionizing the attitude of mind in the entire country, indeed of other countries, as to women's place." At the age of 75, and suffering from cancer, Mrs. Gilman decided the time had come. She left a note that explained her action, concluding with, "Believing the choice to be of social service in promoting wiser views on this question, I have preferred chloroform to cancer."

Her act provoked both cautious praise and some criticism. The woman's stature lent dignity to her decision. Even so, at least one newspaper headlined the story "Charlotte Gilman Dies to Avoid Pain" although her note had accented service. Saying that "human life consists in mutual service," she expressed the opinion that "no grief, pain, misfortune or 'broken heart' is excuse for cutting off one's life while any power of service remains."

In addition to the possible final service of leaving life in a way that might promote a more enlightened view, Mrs. Gilman also left with her literary agent the manuscript for an article that she said could be published after her death. It appeared in *Forum,* titled "The Right To Die," and the *Forum* editors followed the publication with discussion in the subsequent issue by two doctors who took opposing views of the "right to die." Mrs. Gilman's article still reads well. She deplored the advocacy of pain and suffering on the excuse that these are part of God's plan and remarked that "astonishing calumnies have been believed of God." She wrote of the spirit of the old country doctor found dead in his bed with a revolver by his side and the brief note, "There's no damn cancer going to get ahead of me!" Mrs. Gilman wrote also of the "worthwhile life" and said that "the record of a previously noble life is precisely what makes it sheer insult to allow death in pitiful degradation. We may not wish to 'die with our boots on' but we may well prefer to die with our brains on."

The final part of Mrs. Gilman's article outlined the possible procedures by which she believed voluntary euthanasia could become a legally and socially acceptable procedure. She concluded with the prediction that "Instead of being hardened by such measures of release, we shall develop a refinement of tenderness which will shrink with horror at the thought of the suffering and waste we now calmly endure."

The follow-up article in defense of Mrs. Gilman's position was titled "Legalize Euthanasia," and the doctor-author ended with the statement that he personally would insist on euthanasia if he reached a certain condition.

Against the proposal was an article titled "Life Is Sacred," arguing strongly that suffering is good for

30

the human being. "It is not pain but the yielding to self-pity that brings men and women to the point where they take their own lives," the author wrote, but there are others—"heroic men and women" who face it calmly and "are made heroes by the suffering to which they are subjected."

Mrs. Gilman was a better writer than prophet. In her suicide note she said, "Public opinion is changing on this subject. The time is approaching when we shall consider it abhorrent to our civilization to allow a human being to lie in prolonged agony which we should mercifully end in any other creature." She could not guess at the prolongation of "life" that would befall such famous people as Eleanor Roosevelt, Dwight D. Eisenhower and Francisco Franco.

Public opinion—or at least *expressed* public opinion—has changed little in the four decades since Mrs. Gilman's death. Suicide still is a crime in a few of our states; aiding and abetting a suicide is a crime in many states; churchmen of varying faiths continue to regard it as a sin. Suicide is still covered up, whispered over, concealed when possible.

Yet history has demonstrated that almost any view of suicide is possible. A rational and accepting attitude is easily argued. We need only reject the sin-and-crime syndrome and decide that suicide is a good and desirable thing under certain circumstances. Having decided, we should say so.

31

3

THE BALANCE SHEET—
PROFIT AND LOSS

AN elderly woman, once an editor and writer, who built up to her suicide over a number of years, described in a letter left for friends the progress of her thinking and the criteria she used in judging the proper time. One of the friends was John Fischer who told her story in his *Easy Chair* page in *Harper's* in February 1973. "I want to go while I can still enjoy my friends who are so good to me and who I know can still enjoy me," she wrote, "while I can still feel a not too unfavorable balance between happiness and competence and interest and even limited usefulness of my days—and the difficulties and discomforts and pain and expense involved in trying first to maintain that balance and then later merely to prolong life."

This balance, whose weights on either side must differ with each individual, has been recognized as a factor in seemingly logical suicides. A German psychiatrist, Alfred Hoche, gave them a name in

1919 with the term "Bilanz-Selbstmord" or balance-sheet suicide. The label recognized that it was possible for a sane person, thinking logically, to set off the unacceptable or intolerable aspects of his or her life against the chances for betterment and find the result weighted on the side of death.

Although there can be no statistics on such suicides, one guesses their numbers are increasing. It must be added that no researcher has been anxious to look for such common-sense suicides. Because the whole weight of sociological research is on factors to enhance prevention, there is little impetus to find or explain successful or "justified" cases. Again, the sin-and-crime associations seem to frighten investigators away from those cases that defy classification as abnormal. It must also be said that common-sense suicides, like other successes, leave no defeated victims behind to be interviewed.

Balance-sheet suicide inevitably involves a factor of age unless there is severe disability or incurable disease. Young people can, and constantly do, believe that death is dictated because of failed exams, a disappointing love affair, some financial loss or career setback. They do not draw up a balance sheet. If they think they do, the entries they make one day are susceptible to radical change the next.

The elderly have an easier task. If there is one thing we learn in growing old, it is the rarity of reversals. Reversals of a sort are not impossible: a   33

76-year-old woman finds a man interested in her and she blooms—briefly. A woman near retirement age who fears being fired is instead promoted to a better job; she is invigorated. When the circumstances change—in a year, or five, or ten—these women will be like the majority of their contemporaries who did not have the brief and pleasant experience of a reversal of aging. Generally the process is dependable: failing vision does not brighten; wrinkles do not tighten; joint pains may come and go, but they don't go for long.

We all have variations in our way of aging, each with different levels of tolerance for the process. One person's balance sheet will tip in favor of death much earlier than another's. For many, the tipping point will never come. A woman who has had a hard life and innumerable tests of her endurance may be able to face more of the same with an equanimity unavailable to one with less conditioning.

The importance of a "sense of competence" in elderly suicide decisions is recognized. Maurice L. Farber (author of *Theory of Suicide* and many other writings on the subject) mentions that the mother of a Danish friend, "a matriarch of apparently strong character, committed suicide without having any acute difficulties but suffering only from a decline in her formidable powers." The contrast between what one is and was, or the difference between the goals once cherished and the recognized impossibility of attaining them—all go into the balance sheet.

34

Such factors will be subject to frequent change and revision. The death of friends can be important. ("Only a year ago the four of us got together for Marie's birthday. Now I'm the only one left.") Or family changes—the separation of a son and his wife and the removal of grandchildren to some distant point.

Even the trivial can become of scale-tipping importance on occasion. "I never order a green salad when I eat out any more," a 70-year-old woman confided to a friend. "I don't find my mouth properly with a forkful of greens and the dressing drips on my chin. It's embarrassing. A few more of these things and I've had it. You feel such changes . . ."

"I want to go before I get into the food-hiding act," a cheerfully plump woman told her bridge-table friends.

"Oh-oh. Grandma's at it again? What was it this time?"

"Pancake syrup—in a drawer of lingerie. A loose top of course. I have to leave them loose or she can't open them. Well, you wouldn't *believe* the mess." She laughed, but added, "I *mean* it—I hope I'm gone by 70. No, make that 65. I'm sure I'm the food-hiding type."

"Oh, Helen, you get so specific," one of the companions said. "I can remember when you were determined to die by age 35. Let's get on with the game."

General laughter greeted this gem from the past.   35

COMMON-SENSE SUICIDE

They all picked up their cards. Helen looked
thoughtful and briefly unhappy. "I'd forgotten that,
if I really said it . . ."

"You said it. Come on now. What's your bid?"

Failing memory scares a lot of us. "Yes, that
would be a big thing in my balance sheet," a late-
60's woman who still works in an executive position
says. She adds with a half-smile, "That is, if I could
remember to enter it." So long as she can joke about
it, the failing of memory may not be too close. But
she is aware of the danger and probably tries to plan
what to do about it. "I write myself a dozen notes
a day," she says, with another smile. Then she
abruptly changes the subject.

I am glad she does, for her words have called up
a picture of a relative who had a lovely sturdy yel-
low-buff tom cat that had been in the family for
years. Finally only she and Tiger, the tom, were left
in the big frame house in the small town. She clung
to the house and to her independence while her
memory failed. The rooms of the house began to be
plastered with notes—and one out of five would say
something like "feed cat," "get cat food," "look for
cat food." Only now and then, in a particularly clear
moment, one assumes, did she remember Tiger's
name and then a note might say "Tiger likes kidney
—order some." In the end it was a half-starved
Tiger who alerted a neighbor by climbing up the
draperies of a sunny dining room window where

36

uncared-for plants were dying in their pots. The neighbor called the local minister and they investigated. The badly undernourished woman was taken to a nursing home; Tiger was put to sleep, as the saying goes. Lucky Tiger.

Health entries, both physical and mental, would come first and carry a big part of the weight in the average balance sheet. Family and friends might come next, and economic factors after that. Economic factors, with many, would come second regardless of the presence or absence of family and friends.

Those who spend their time with the elderly report two overwhelming preoccupations among them: health and solvency. The two are inextricably tied. Inflation has dissolved into quicksand the foundations under the most careful and cautious economic plans of the retired. Even Medicare and Medicaid, which are unbelievably generous in terms of what many present senior citizens might ever have expected, still do not assure sufficient care, nor do they allow much element of choice to those who still feel competent to manage their own lives. A prolonged illness now can bankrupt even a wealthy person. For the elderly poor, the fear of such an illness is an ever-present terror.

The average ailing older person who has a pension, an annuity, a trust fund, investments, savings, real property—any or all of these—must face a time 37 when a frying-pan or fire choice has to be made. If there is no family situation into which the person can fit, with reasonable financial justice for all, then a type of security must be bought with whatever assets remain. This often means turning over property and assigning social security and pension payments to a retirement home that, in turn, undertakes to see its clients through to the end. If available assets are too limited, many of the same institutions accept residents who, when their funds run out, will have to depend on Medicaid. Medicaid-bolstered institutions vary from excellent to horrible. In urban centers, particularly, they can be places of incredible inhumanity. Those institutions with a reasonably good reputation, often associated with religious or fraternal orders, may have long waiting lists.

Whether the specific retirement home is good or bad, its doors close with equal finality on a client's assets. Alternative arrangements, where the elderly hire private care within their own homes, often are equally expensive and equally unsatisfactory. Private-arrangement care also is less permanent—an interim solution that gives way to institutional care later on. In whatever way the change of life style may be handled, through one big step or a series of changes, the golden years for the less-than-healthy older person effectively consume the gold that might have gone in quite another direction.

38   Two men overheard in conversation on a com-

muter bus discussed their mothers. "It'll be two years tomorrow she's been in that home," one of them said. "And poor mom thinks she's still got those twelve hundred shares of AT&T."

"Her mind's okay, then?"

"No, no. Her mind's half gone. But she remembers AT&T—doesn't remember selling it, just having it. I guess it gave her comfort for so long she still leans on it. Real financial security." He laughed, briefly and half-bitterly.

"Yeah. Well, maybe it's better that way," his companion said. "My wife's mother still has all her buttons and she worries about every dime that's going down the drain. She was going to help Jeff through law school—and she remembers that. It's terrible to see her feel guilty about it."

"Sure. That's even worse."

Statistics on individual cases of medical care in which bills have amounted to hundreds of thousands of dollars for a comatose, hopeless, long-living invalid are common enough. One such situation, going on for almost eight years, cost close to $300,000. Another reference cites almost $29,000 for the final 16 days of the life of a heart transplant patient, plus another $7000 worth of blood. Yet another citation refers to an accident victim—with irrecoverable injuries and $160,000 worth of care before she died. Sylvia Porter said, in a 1976 column, that hospital bills of $70,000 are "commonplace" these days.

Worse than the tremendous individual bill is the sum of those that are only relentlessly average. A middle-aged aide whose duties were mainly with eight patients on one corridor of a suburban nursing home became familiar with their situations. Three of the women had no relatives in the area. Two of these had been career women who used up their resources and were on Medicaid except for their social security. They suffered from crippling arthritis and a heart condition. The third, mildly senile, had a niece in another state who had power-of-attorney and made payments from available funds. She came twice (during the aide's time on the job) to see the aunt. "She was dressed like money—maybe they can afford it. And she was nice. Too bad her aunt didn't know who she was."

Three of the other five—one in a wheelchair with a broken hip, one with advanced emphysema, one senile—had relatives who visited "fairly often" and among these visitors one couple appeared financially well off. Another, a daughter of a patient, looked "weak and sick and sometimes she cries." This daughter got particularly upset if there was need for any special attention that would entail an additional charge. "She must be the one who pays," because none of these three were on public funding so far.

The other two women were on Medicaid funds and were long-term cases although neither was senile. One was partially paralyzed; the other had a

40

bone disease that would not respond to treatment. Both had some family but no regular visitors. "I think they're good enough people," the aide defended them. "But they're hard up. They work— and it's not easy to come out here from the city. A little girl came and danced at a Christmas program. Great granddaughter I'd guess. The old lady was real proud of her—told everybody."

That was the only comment about any kind of enjoyment of life in this eight-bed corridor. The sum of pain, confusion and discontent was evident. ("She has some bad nights. Sometimes the medicines help and then they wear off and before they have her on something else she might have nightmares or get afraid of something . . ." And of the woman whose niece "dressed like money": "Sometimes she thinks guests are going to spend the night —like this whole place was her house or something. She won't want to go to bed because she says she's given this room to a guest and she plans to sleep somewhere else. Whoever's on that night may have to take her for a little walk so she forgets it, and then bring her back to her own bed.") If no one has time for "a little walk," or if during that walk some of the other seven charges of one attendant have special needs, the care of course must be rationed. In this particular place, one felt, the ration probably was well above average.

The sum of the fees for such an eight-bed corridor   41

COMMON-SENSE SUICIDE

can be computed at about $3000 a week. The time-
span for occupancy by each of these eight women
was open-ended. Ten such corridors make up an
average nursing home ($30,000). Fifteen thousand
homes stretch across our land ($450 million). A year
of $450-million-dollar weeks is a $23-billion-dollar
year. What do we get for this $23-billion price tag?
One thing we *don't* get is a green light at the end of
the corridor.

Those of us who end up disabled and in our right
minds may feel forced to make a moral choice between obeying or circumventing some of the rules
of institutional retirement. If we have family members who need and depend on some help from us,
it often is necessary to plan ahead, anticipate the
worst, and arrange a transfer of funds and property
titles within the legal limits. Such maneuvering,
which allows us to approach the institution more or
less emptyhanded, is common practice. It also is
distasteful to the people of whom it is most likely to
be required. It does not apply to the very rich or the
very poor, but to the big middle class of people who
budget and save and who could sincerely believe, at
one time, in their ability to take care of themselves
and to be thriftily generous with others close to
them.

Whether we turn early or late to public aid, however, the majority of us will draw down a sizable
amount from Medicare and Medicaid on our way to

42

the receding nearest exit. Medicare, the health insurance scheme that is part of the Social Security Administration, is primarily for the 65-up group of Americans. (The under-65 disabled beneficiaries of the program numbered only 2.1 million persons in mid-1975 out of a Medicare total of 24.6 million.) The program was inaugurated in the mid-1960s and the annual payout by 1971–1972 was $6.1 billion; by 1975–1976 the figures had risen to $12.4 billion. An assurance that the figures will continue to rise, and at a steeper rate, is contained not only in anticipated inflation but also in the fact that at least a thousand people are added to the 65-up population *every day*. About 4000 enter this golden-age area of our population daily; about 3000 depart. The net daily gain of one thousand, looked on statistically as aging bodies qualified for Medicare, is hardly a cause for fiscal celebration. Older Americans required a per capita health-care expenditure of $1360 in 1975 against one-third of that amount for younger people. Two-thirds of the $1360 was paid through public programs.

Medicaid, the program of health care for all needy persons regardless of age, with both federal and state funding, also spends billions annually on the older population. Long-term nursing home residence, except for the relatively well-to-do, usually depends on Medicaid (nursing home time under Medicare is strictly limited). About 80% of nursing home patients receive Medicaid funds and the average stay in a nursing home is three years.

Whether these final years are paid for in private or public dollars, the bill must be paid. If the patient is mentally confused, the nursing-home stay can be, at best, a foggy and meaningless experience. At worst, of course, it can be torture. For the mentally alert, it is (quite apart from all other discomforts) a time when one must watch the rapid outflow of funds while being aware of all the things one would prefer to see the money applied to.

A decade ago, at a West Coast seminar on the subject of suicide, one of the informed speakers estimated that the saving of three persons from self-destruction would be worth one hundred thousand dollars to the community. This estimate was based on the assumption that the saved person would be an earner and a taxpayer; the figure was modest. The suicide of a nonproductive person with failing health is an entry for the other side of this public balance sheet. Her, or his, departure can hardly fail to be an asset to the community. If the suicide was a solvent taxpayer, taxes will be levied on the estate; if indigent, the government is spared further expense on a life basically finished. For the just-solvent in-betweens, the younger members of the family may benefit in a modest way, either through inheritance or by being spared the burden of further expense. The biggest dividends—which cannot be calculated mathematically—come in the curtailment of human misery.

One figure no aging person can afford to ignore is the ever-rising cost to each productive worker for his share of the burden of the elderly. ("Burden" is used more and more candidly in this connection; the press appears to find it no longer offensive.) Our expanded programs, with or without the expensive abuses that make them an even greater luxury, have to be paid for by the earning segment of our society. Our earners are, in theory, willing to share our total national product with the unproductive old because they understand that they themselves will grow old and require benefits. Nevertheless, a society aging as fast as ours is likely to impose a greater burden than some younger people will blandly accept. Already, the FICA (Social Security) deductions on many wage-earners' pay checks are far larger than income tax deductions. The FICA payments are unavoidable, applying to minimum wages as well as to the first specific few thousands ($16,500 in 1977) of a corporate executive's or TV star's high pay. Even so, the Social Security system operates at a deficit and faces long-term insolvency unless it is overhauled. In the overhauling, some basic decisions on how much the productive sector can afford to share with the unproductive will have to be made.

A well-known management consultant, speaking to a group of top business executives at a 1976 sym-

45

posium sponsored by New York University's graduate school of business administration, stated that the "central concern" of economic planners in all developed nations from now on will have to be the growing burden of support for people who are past working age.

In the history of suicide, the shift from self-destruction as an aspect of individual morality to self-destruction as a social phenomenon coincided with the industrial revolution. In a way, the suicide became at that point a soulless early statistic in a readjusting economic society. Today, the needs of the individual and those of the social community appear to merge, in an economic sense, on the question of old-age suicide. A planned departure that serves oneself, one's family and also the state surely is worthy of decent consideration.

A Frenchman who was a retired railway worker planned his suicide four years in advance and pro rated his assets of four million francs through those years. He had good friends and good hobbies (fishing and cooking) and was a locally noted raconteur who told adventure stories of his past experience in the Cameroons. He was busy, well-liked, apparently happy in the environment of his village. The four years ended with the man in obvious good health—and with a sceptical attitude evident on the part of his friends about the seriousness of his intent. But he meant it. The note he left, after taking an

46

overdose of sleeping pills, said, "I am punctual. I think I've lived better than others. I die content."

This man was only 60—having opted at age 56 for more of the "good life" in less years than he might normally anticipate. Although there is nothing typical about his circumstances, his story indicates that there are some who prefer to go too early rather than too late.

Most of us will have more serious worries than how to preserve a bit of the good life with dwindling resources. Those worries would be relieved to some extent if we knew that, after careful planning and putting things in order, we could tote up our balance sheet, interpret the result and act on our own decision.

Psychiatrists can tell us various things about the personality of suicides. One opinion is that the suicide often is a person who likes to be in control. In the ferment of today's society, people who prefer being in control—which means self-control in the case of suicide—are assets.

There are going to be more than thirty million American senior citizens by the year 2000. More than two million of them will be in nursing homes —perhaps double the current number. Those who have the will to opt out may not (yet) get a public vote of thanks. But who can dare say that they will be missed?

4

SUICIDE AND THE LAW

THE individual's importance to the state was long the rationale for the ban on self-slaughter. Slaves and soldiers, with a demonstrable role to play, were prohibited from ending their own lives under Roman law. A suspected criminal whose suicide would allow him to avoid trial for any crime that could be punished by forfeiture of his estate also was prohibited from killing himself. In such an instance the suspect would be declared to be without legal heirs. Relatives nevertheless were allowed to defend the deceased as if he were still living—and if he was found innocent they retained his worldly goods.

The legal view of suicide has appeared to become less rational over time. State church precepts linked sin and crime so inextricably that even in the eighteenth century Blackstone could state that "the suicide is guilty of a double offence: one spiritual, in evading the prerogative of the Almighty, and rushing into his immediate presence uncalled for; the other temporal, against the King, who hath an interest in the preservation of all his subjects."

English law retained forfeiture as a punishment until 1870 and did not remove the criminal stigma from attempted suicide until 1961. Defense of the legal censure usually rested on the belief that the sin and crime associations with suicide acted as a deterrent—and of course on the assumption that a deterrent was desirable.

This view was brought by the colonists to our shores. The Massachusetts legislature, in 1660, went on record as declaring that God called on them "to bear testimony against such wicked and unnatural practices, that others may be deterred therefrom." The legislators enacted a law requiring that self-murderers be denied a grave among Christians and be buried "in some common highway . . . and a cartload of stones laid upon the grave, as a brand of infamy and as a warning to others to beware of the like damnable practices."

Defilement as a deterrent was at least minimally defensible at a time when the new world needed every productive person. Few people reached unproductive old age under the rigors of colonial life. By the eighteenth century, several voices questioned the basis for laws against suicide. The French political philosopher Montesquieu (in his *Persian Letters*) held that society is founded on mutual advantage and that the individual has no obligation to

49

refrain from suicide when that advantage ceases to exist. An updating of this opinion could stress the "mutual" factor and recognize that neither the individual *or* the society departed from loses much advantage because of the elderly suicide.

Most of the legal questions now connected with suicide do not concern the elderly. The payment of life insurance claims, for instance, often is the subject of a court suit by a suicide's beneficiary. Most policies require a one- or two-year period before they become effective in suicide cases and most accident and health policies exclude suicide and suicide attempts (during which disabling "accidents" often occur) from their coverage. Proving or disproving suicidal intent versus accident in cases that may qualify for double indemnity is also a matter often taken to court.

The elderly are excluded from most of these insurance problems because, if insured, they either have held their policies for many years or have some modest amount of special senior citizen coverage—too small for an insurance company to argue about. Even in cases of injury through attempted suicide, the elderly person presumably will live long enough to draw down only a limited number of benefit payments. It would be difficult for an elderly person to defraud an insurance company by taking out a large policy prior to a planned suicide. The intended suicide would have to pay exorbitant premiums during the two-year period or else would have to plan so far ahead that "old age" would hardly be a factor.

Over all, the insurance companies do not appear to have much of a problem with suicide. Although the U.S. suicide rate increased by about 8% in the 1965 to 1975 decade, the rate among one large company's policyholders decreased by 7% in the same period. Policyholders are both healthier and wealthier than the general population mix. In addition, much of our suicide increase is among the young, many of whom are uninsured.

Even the aggregate life insurance payout figures on death by suicide have grown surprisingly little— or have actually decreased when one takes inflation into account. A rough estimate in 1932 gave a suicide-claims figure of $75 million for all insurance companies in the U.S.A. The Institute of Life Insurance arrives at a payout estimate of $80.5 million in 1975 under "ordinary" life insurance benefits by all companies. "Ordinary" life insurance (as distinguished from group, industrial, etc.) represents only 51% of total life insurance in the U.S.—but even a doubling of the $80.5 million figure does not approach the real value of $75 million in 1932 dollars.

I think it is safe to say that insurance company actuaries will keep up with the times in their rate-setting and that the beneficiaries of elderly policyholders, suicides or not, will collect without extraordinary problems. Nevertheless, any legislation that aims at erasing legal barriers or stigma associated with suicide should provide for nondiscriminatory treatment in insurance benefits (just as such clauses are included in proposed euthanasia bills and in the recently passed California right-to-die bill).

Workmen's compensation cases, wherein judges and juries are required to decide to what extent a work-related disability may have led a person to suicide, also are outside the probable experience of most elders. Nor are we likely to depart under such circumstances that our suicide can be seen as evidence of guilt—a common assumption in criminal law in the past. Daniel Webster, arguing a murder case in 1830, stated that "There is no refuge from confession but suicide; and suicide is confession."

The elderly suicide confesses only that the absence of life has become more attractive than its presence. She or he confesses an impatience with the slow process of modern dying. And in most legal connections, the view of others is that something that would have happened soon has happened a little bit sooner.

All this is not to say that the older person who considers suicide has no concern with the law. We have a primary interest in promoting the complete decriminalization of the aiding and abetting of a suicide and exemption from any conspiracy charges that may be brought against a survivor of suicide "pacts" or agreements. Although the romantic pic-

52

ture of a suicide pact may involve dewy-eyed young lovers, actual suicide agreements (and efforts) are much more common among the old. Many husband-and-wife couples decide on mutual-aid suicides— probably many more than find their way into either the statistics or the news. They become newsworthy when something goes wrong. And they often also become court cases when something goes wrong. The survivor in an incomplete suicide pact may be, and sometimes is, accused of murder. In many states, aiding and abetting is considered manslaughter. Attendant circumstances, likely to produce no witnesses other than the survivor, can be interpreted as quite damning. There may be only the verbal assurance of the survivor of the pact that any pact existed, or the existence of a pact may in itself be criminal conspiracy. Drug-induced deaths, in which the same supposed lethal dosage of a drug kills one person but sends the other only into a coma—and then into a hospital—are fairly common. The coroner's duty, in such cases, is to question the circumstances.

A researcher who investigated 58 cases of uncompleted suicide pacts, 42 of them involving married couples, found that one of the partners usually conceives the idea and influences the other to go along. If the one who "went along" fails to complete the suicidal act, possibly out of unconscious reluctance to succeed, she or he may stand accused of manslaughter. The variations, of course, are many.　53

In cases of mutual agreement by unrelated persons, an incomplete suicide may appear even more suspicious. The question also has been raised whether, in jurisdictions where attempted suicide is still a felony, a person who is aware of the attempt has a legal obligation to take action to prevent the felony.

Although prosecutions for aiding and abetting suicide are not common, they are frequent enough to make legal reform a practical rather than a theoretical concern. In 1975 a 65-year-old Michigan man (a retired educator) was convicted of manslaughter, after a no-contest plea, in connection with the carbon monoxide death of his wife, also 65. He was put on 30 months' probation and fined $3750. Possible miscarriages of justice in similar cases will be avoided only when legal provision is made for willing suicides to record their intentions. Only then can the motives of friends or relatives be unclouded by doubt.

The situation of the mentally incompetent elderly person may require more than a prerecorded intention, if that intention actually is to be carried out. A strong argument can be made for the right of a person, at any age, to appoint a personal guardian, or "committee of the person," as it has been called, to make a decision that in all likelihood would be made by the "person" herself or himself if the person were mentally capable. Instructions set down well in advance of likely senility or other impairment, specifying the limits of incapacity beyond which one does not choose to survive, could serve as a reliable guide. Actions taken by the responsible person or persons, on the basis of such guidance, would be not only tolerated but legally protected. Many states have laws that allow fairly wide discretion on the part of guardians of property. There could, and we hope there will, come a time when such legally constituted authority can help a confused elderly sufferer to dispose of life no less harmoniously than of property.

The seeming backwardness of the law has been compensated for, to some extent, by leniency on the part of judges and juries. However, such leniency often can be exercised only by ascribing insanity to the person who has tried but failed to end his or her life. In England the law distinguishes between *"felo de se"* (felony upon self) and "suicide," with the former requiring intent—and therefore sanity. The "suicide," then, is *ipso facto non compos mentis.* English coroner's juries, before the Suicide Act of 1961 that decriminalized attempts, found less than two percent of attempted suicides to be *felo de se.* But the label of insanity was the price the 98% had to pay.

Public opinion, as demonstrated in English coroner's juries and our own evasions (the attribution of mental unbalance often provides an out for both our courts and churches), is ahead of the law. We need, at this point, to go further than decriminalization (important as that is) and make legal provisions that will eliminate the need for evasive tactics to protect the suicide's right of self-termination. There will be many arguments against this—arguments similar to those opposing legal euthanasia, for the two are closely related. There are advocates of a "let things be" stand, who point out that doctors and other medical personnel quietly ease the way out of life for many people and that it is best left so. Doctors, this opinion holds, are better to be trusted with the decision than any administrative group acting on a set of legal rules.

This argument is really not defensible. It ignores the medical practitioners' own right to decide against the role of executioner; it ignores the reality of the unsettled question of massive malpractice suits; it leaves the stigma on both euthanasia and suicide by refusing them examination in the legal light of day.

These questions deserve full examination. "Safeguarding a person's right to die when and as he chooses," says Professor Horace M. Kallen (speaking at a symposium on Morals, Medicine and Law), "so long as this right works no violence on the rights of others, seems to me a proper function for the laws of a free society of free and educated men."

The close relationship between suicide and euthanasia was pointed up by a bill introduced in the British Parliament in 1970 (and defeated). Advocates of the bill argued that euthanasia could be legalized merely by amending the Suicide Act of 1961 to eliminate aiding and abetting as an offense. In other words, euthanasia would be simply aiding and abetting suicide, and aiding and abetting would not be criminal. Doctors and religious representatives both opposed this approach because of the "executioner" implication. However, supporters of the bill brought up the valid point that voluntary euthanasia could eliminate the unsatisfactory outcome of many attempted suicides and thus save much misery—especially for the old.

The ancient Greeks made provision for legal suicide. Precepts, as reported by Libanius, were clearly stated:

Whoever no longer wishes to live shall state his reasons to the Senate. . . . If your existence is hateful to you . . . if you are overwhelmed by fate . . . bowed with grief, abandon life. Let the unhappy man recount his misfortune, let the magistrate supply him with the remedy, and his wretchedness will come to an end.

The Athenian law also applied at Ceos and was transplanted to Marseilles by the Greek colonists. Magistrates kept a supply of poison on hand and dispensed it in the proper dosage to those who had received authorization for their suicide.

Surely our twentieth century legislators, with our 57

persistent encouragement, can find a way to catch up with the Greeks on this humane issue.

Meanwhile, our not-too-patient encouragement might take the form of aiding and abetting the "protective ambiguity" that sometimes surrounds the demise of a suffering patient. Medical personnel, on the urgent pleas of patient or family or both, sometimes takes steps to hasten the desired end. These steps, under present laws, must be cautious indeed.

Good friends of an elderly patient may, on occasion, be in a position to help out. If a terminal, suffering woman is visited by four or five contemporaries on her final day, much confusion and protective ambiguity will color that day. Did one of the visitors slip her a fatal pill? Did some of them pester her doctor enough to interfere with his routine? Did the nurse get confused when one of the visitors had a fainting spell and asked for help? I do not see a group of elderly women taken to court to explain one empty bed that had been occupied by their good friend.

If a family turns to friends of the suffering patient, to ask for any kind of aid, we do not risk much in giving it. We risk no career, as do members of the medical staff. We risk no intrafamily controversy that may leave a trail of guilt and hard feelings. We risk no guilt within ourselves because we would not come to our friend's aid if we did not believe in the rightness of doing so.

58

If we believe in the rightness of a suicide-permitting law and regret the slow coming of such a law, many of us can justify a bit of underground nudging. We also can rise to the defense of any doctor or staff member of a medical facility who is accused of an aiding-and-abetting action that we would hope might be available to us under the same circumstances. Clearly stated support by the elderly themselves can help to provide legal sanction for the human impulses that too often are stifled.

5

SUICIDE AND THE CHURCHES

No matter how or when the legalization of old-age suicide may come about, many who are tempted will continue to be deterred by religious beliefs. The awesomeness of the idea of "God-given life" persists almost as stubbornly as our durable old bodies. The sanctity of life, regardless of the condition of that "life," is being defended on various fronts and will continue to be defended. But opposition to orthodox sanctity-of-life views also is strong, both within and without the various religious communities. The changing status of divorce, contraception and abortion (at a time when a religious revival also is noted) shows a trend toward new church-vocabulary definitions in relation to many moral and ethical questions of today's society.

As we noted in the brief history of suicide, the church has made major adjustments in the past—with Christianity saving itself from possible extinction through martyrdom—and there is no reason to doubt that necessary adjustment will continue. If we anticipate that the pace of this adjustment will be too slow for our personal tastes, however, we can find reasons to move to the forefront of religious thinking.

A 1927 article on suicide (from *Survey,* May 15, 1927) came close to dismissing the religious factor altogether, saying: "The old appeal that suicide was of the devil, and hence abhorrent, rested on a type of religion now practically extinct and totally out of harmony with present trends of thought." Unfortunately, that "old appeal" is still heard fifty years later. It sounds ever more illogical, but it can be useful. It can remind us how out of proportion, in a scientific versus social sense, the changes of the past fifty years have been. It can warn us about possible dangers in 2027. It can nudge us to update our "beliefs" by reexamining their source, their validity and their suitability.

Pre-Christian religions viewed suicide as a privilege earned by the mature, the wise and the holy. It usually was condemned for the ordinary person. In Hinduism, the *Rigveda* provided the doctrine that an old man has the privilege and duty to adopt a hermit's life-style (i.e., to be no burden on his sons) unless he prefers to terminate his existence. Hinduism afforded a variety of laudable means for suicide—hurling oneself from a sacred mountain, finding mystic union with the gods by drowning at the confluence of the holy Jumna and Ganges rivers, or dying under the wheels of the cart that carried the image of Jagannath (incarnation of Vishnu) at the annual festival in Puri. Humbler suicides also are described in Hindu lore. One story tells how a hunter in the forest encountered a bird who roasted himself as an offering to the guest. The bird's wife, in sadness, refused to live without her husband and took her own life. The hunter, touched by the sacrifice of the pair, then killed himself by burning. All, of course, from lowly to holy, would return to the wheel and take up again the burden of life in various incarnations.

Jainism, in which all life is revered (even to the point of a person's wearing a mask lest his breath destroy an insect), nevertheless accepted suicide as the reward for supreme asceticism. Starvation, the logical outcome of protracted fasting, was the final ascetic act.

Buddhism, which condemns asceticism, also condemns suicide—both are contrary to the goal of indifference to life or death. Buddhist doctrine has specifically said that one cannot get to Nirvana by suicide. Despite this statement, the extensive Buddhist literature is full of suicides, many of which come at the moment of enlightenment. Some of the Buddhist saints had the power to "loosen the *samskaras* of life" at will, but those who did not could "take to the sword" when they had achieved what they set out to do. A Buddhist statement says of a sacrificial death: "To give one's body is better than to give alms; . . . to burn one's body as an offering is certainly more meritorious than to kindle lamps at a shrine."

Shintoism, which combined elements of animism, Confucianism and Buddhism, regarded suicide as a privilege to be earned and, in time, formalized the act into an elaborate ritual.

The big dividing line between the Oriental religions and the later Judeo-Christian and Moslem religions is not merely the monotheism of the latter but also the contrast between repeated reincarnations and a single life with a promised afterlife. No matter that the reincarnations were seen as burdens to be borne and worked off in a slow progression toward the bliss of nonbeing—they still represented a permanency of second chances. In the context of suicide this contrast is important. The attainment of a happy afterlife (or its alternative of eternal hell) is a one-chance thing that, once believed in, is not easily relinquished or rethought. If suicide, the unrepentable sin, closes the door to everafter bliss, dare one risk it?

Like any other risk, this one needs careful scrutiny. Qualifications for the afterlife have been, and surely will continue to be, redefined and modified by all faiths.

Christians and Jews are supposed to forego self-slaughter on the basis of "Thou shalt not kill," and

Moslems on the instruction, "It is not for a believer to kill a believer except by mistake . . . and whoso kills a believer purposely, his reward is hell." A believer who kills himself is, of course, killing a believer, but the wording at least allows a coverage for *jihad,* the holy war. Lacking such coverage, the Christian and Jewish faiths have nevertheless managed to accommodate the death-dealing requirements of war.

Also, the histories of all the faiths are spattered with exceptions to the suicide ban—often exceptions that obviously arouse pride in the faithful of whatever faith. Some of the Catholic saints were suicides, including women who chose death to protect their virginity. And when celibacy for the priesthood was decreed (in the eleventh century), wives of priests sometimes chose to die. The Koranic bar to Moslem suicides did not impede heroic self-sacrifice in holy wars of the past nor the turning-upon-self of modern terrorist weapons today. Suicides were frequent, too, among both Moslem and Hindu women to escape the terrors of the 1947 partition riots and mass migrations that accompanied the formation of free India and Pakistan. The Jewish prohibition accommodated suicide in defense of the Torah. And the mass suicide at Masada, where 960 men, women and children chose death over surrender to the Romans after three years of siege, is recalled with pride by modern Jewry. Only two women and five children survived this largest of suicide pacts to tell the story of Masada.

A modern example of accommodation by the church, in this case the Roman Catholic, is the problem of Irish terrorists who starved themselves to death in British jails. A Benedictine monk who wrote to the London *Times* on the subject in 1974 said:

It seems clear to me that the hunger strikers . . . are, on Catholic principles, engaged in a gravely sinful course of action. Accordingly, I do not see how any Roman Catholic priest can give holy communion or absolution or Christian burial to any of the hunger strikers. I deplore the failure of the Roman Catholic hierarchy to explain the intrinsic immorality of what these brave but muddled and misguided young people are doing . . .

This apparently was a minority opinion, for a requiem mass and funeral procession were held soon after for a convicted IRA terrorist who had starved himself to death. One publication, analyzing the circumstances of the event, commented that the Church based its stand on a "highly convoluted argument." By and large, one can say that highly convoluted arguments are available whenever the tide of public opinion forms a hard-to-resist force.

This day will come for euthanasia and for suicide. Until it arrives, we can ask our own questions.

If you want to question where the religious ban 65

on suicide came from and why it persists, you will
not be alone, nor will you be very original. Arthur
Schopenhauer, in the early 1800s, put it strongly
(even though he was against suicide):

I am of the opinion that the clergy should once and for
all be challenged to give an account with what right they,
without being able to show any Biblical authority, or any
valid philosophical arguments, stigmatize in the pulpit
and in their writings an action committed by many . . .
and refuse those who voluntarily leave this world, an
honorable burial . . .

A century and a half later, no satisfactory and satisfy-
ing reasons emerge from pulpits or church papers.

One of the *un*satisfactory reasons put forward is
the value of suffering. The Christian faith habitually
has extolled suffering and its "ennobling" effects.
The value-of-suffering theory delayed use of the
early anesthetics, whose developers were attacked
by religious spokesmen for doing the work of the
devil. Catholic spokesmen, even in recent times,
have called suffering "the greatest possible source of
heroism, purification and redemption." But Pope
Pius XII, in 1957, answered three questions on "the
religious and moral implications of pain prevention" in the light of Christian doctrine by apparently
condoning the use of narcotics for the lessening of
66   pain even if such use might shorten life. (This 1957

statement marks the closest approach of the Roman Catholic Church to sanctioning passive euthanasia.)

If the question of suffering comes down to *how much* suffering is good for you, each individual surely is given (or can take) a choice suitable to her or his needs. Job rejected suicide despite his trials. This rejection often has been cited as evidence that the Bible is against suicide, although no such conclusion is implicit in Job's story. We can as easily take the simple message that Job, bolstered by his faith, had an endurance rather beyond our own. (Speaking of suffering, I like the story of the old lady who observed her first anniversary in a hospital bed with the comment, "If God doesn't hurry up and take me I'm going to be too mad to speak to him when he does!")

The analysis of Christ's death on the cross also is variable. Many people, within and without the Church, consider Christ's death a premeditated suicide—a deliberate sacrifice that, given his powers, he certainly could have avoided. Others view this analysis as blasphemy. A recent letter to the *New York Times,* from a monsignor, fulminated against another letter-writer who had cooperated in his wife's suicide in a case of inoperable cancer and who had used the term "death with dignity." The monsignor mentions "cogent legal, medical and social arguments against suicide" and ends with: "Finally, for Christians there is the added undeniable fact that

Jesus Christ did not choose to 'die with dignity.' "

Undeniable fact? There are few of those in any of our circuitously evolved faiths. Again, we may take our choice.

Eternal life, so long a central theme of Christianity, has become less and less believed in. A Gallup poll dating from around 1970 found that one in four of those Americans who professed a belief in God did not believe in his power to raise them or anyone else from the dead. The belief is hard to hang onto in a modern society that allows freedom of investigation to all members and surrounds us with a whirlwind of scientific and technological news and development. Most churches adjust and modify—playing down such themes as eternal life except perhaps for the Easter sermon. The fundamentalist sects who still flatly promise eternal life for the chosen are careful to shield those chosen from the world at large. They specialize in maintaining a close fellowship in which mutual support is always available and contaminating outside influences are spurned.

Probably there is less disorientation or *anomie* among such close-knit groups than in the intellectual circles of modern religion. Several progressive denominations distribute study literature on euthanasia and open the doors of their churches for discussion of humanitarian concepts that do not conflict with their religious beliefs. A hint of things to come is contained in a Catholic writer's reference to "idolatry of life" in connection with sustained life-support efforts. If extraordinary life-prolonging practices can be tagged "idolatry," then the "shalt not kill" commandment, as a prohibition to euthanasia and suicide, will have a rival.

Suicide is not consistently rejected by churchmen, even for themselves. One of the best known "pact" cases was the attempted double suicide of Dr. Henry Pitney Van Dusen and his wife in 1975. Dr. Van Dusen had been president of the Union Theological Seminary and enjoyed world recognition. He and his wife had long supported the concept of voluntary euthanasia and Dr. Van Dusen had gone on record as early as 1946, along with forty other religious leaders, to register that support. Dr. Van Dusen suffered a stroke in 1970 and lost the speaking facility that had been such a large part of his life. His wife was arthritic. Both were becoming more and more dependent on others.

They came to their decision in late January 1975 and both took large doses of sleeping pills. As in many pacts, one succumbed peacefully (Mrs. Van Dusen) but the other did not. Dr. Van Dusen was hospitalized and lived until mid-February. The actual circumstances of the deaths were not made public until after Dr. Van Dusen's passing. Then the couple's simple note was released, and public opinion—both pro and con—had its day. One of the pros suggested that, "Far from being the ultimate failure of liberal Protestantism, it (suicide) is the ultimate triumph." And one of the cons stated that "Our profound sin is to believe that we are 'in charge' and determine our fate and the fate of the world."

The Van Dusens' own note commented that "Nowadays it is difficult to die," and added, "We feel that this way we are taking will become more usual and acceptable as the years pass." One of the thoughtful editorials on the subject (by Norman Cousins in *Saturday Review*, June 14, 1975) asked: "Why are so many people more readily appalled by an unnatural form of dying than by an unnatural form of living?"

Psychologists who specialize in suicide research have noted that a belief in an afterlife has no classifiable effect on suicides. Such a belief appears to inhibit suicide for some and to make it more acceptable to others. Our interference with all sorts of natural phenomena once considered the province of a god or gods has reached such an extent that one doubts if strictly religious considerations, in connection with suicide among other things, are possible for most people today. Scientists not only prolong life almost indefinitely but also have provided, through cryonics, a deep-freeze gamble on immortality for those of massive means (and massive egos). Heavenly bookkeeping on who does or does not deserve an afterlife must be seriously complicated. "God's plan," aided, abetted or aborted by man's interference, remains a mystery.

70

Dare we allege that any god deliberately planned a world made up of overwhelmingly large numbers of young people in areas that are not self-sustaining in food—and then set against these multitudes the richly overfed and ever-aging societies of the developed world? Without effective birth control at one end of this imbalanced picture, and some termination of life at the other, this is the emerging (quickly emerging) design.

Most of us have some small private picture that represents big concepts like overpopulation. Mine is a dual picture. Scene One comes out of India three decades ago when, one scorching afternoon, the persistent sound of a child crying took me outside the house in a half-built development to find the source. A tiny girl, probably a year and a half old, sat in the shade of the house wall, crying with a monotonous dry-eyed kind of despair. Her little hands were knotted into fists the size of walnuts and tied loosely together by a short dirty cord that bit into her wrists. While I stood viewing her in near disbelief—for the Indian people do not torture children—a small crowd gathered to stand by and to comment among themselves, presumably on my interest in this matter. Among the bystanders were construction workers from a house site adjoining mine, and also an English-speaking servant from one of the occupied houses.

One of the workers from the site was a small, strong-bodied girl in her late teens whose job was to

71

carry sand in a head-borne receptacle to the crude
cement-mixer. She began to cry. She tried to hide
her face behind the untucked tail of her sari but the
interpreter-servant spoke sharply to her and explained to me that this girl was the baby's mother.
Conversation of a sort ensued. I learned that the
baby's hands were tied because she ate dirt. It was
not that the mother did not feed her—with defen-
sive gestures the humiliated young woman untied a
small cloth packet at her waist and demonstrated that
the child would not take the grains of parched *dahl*
(split pea) or crumbs of leftover bread. She wanted
to eat dirt.

There probably was no way for the sand-carrying
laborer to understand whatever the self-important
interpreter conveyed of my message that the baby's
insistence on dirt showed a need for some specific
nourishment. I went to get a few rupees for the girl,
who promised to take time off and take her baby to
a clinic. The crowd wandered away. If the baby
cried on the following days, I did not hear her. But
I believe that she cried and I still can call the sound
into memory.

Scene Two is a nursing home in a small U.S. town.
It is a big old house converted to serve the needs of
the community's aging population. I went there to
visit a relative and found her (in good shape after a
minor fall and soon to be released) in one of the
upstairs rooms. When I left, coming down the grace-

ful stairway that curved into the entry hall, the woman in charge of the home was waiting to show me around. She was particularly proud of the old dining room—a large, wide-windowed sunny room with southeast exposure where six beds still allowed room for the easy movement of attendants. Most of the beds were occupied, but one immediately attracted my attention. This bed was placed to catch lots of sun and its white-haired occupant, tidy and clean in a pale blue bedjacket, reclined against a slightly raised pillow. Her hands, outside the folded-down bedcover, lay quietly at her sides. Her eyes were the blue of the jacket and were wide open but staring. She was motionless except for a steady chewing movement that seemed fuelled by something being fed to her out of a brown paper bag by an equally white-haired visitor who stood beside the bed. We moved closer and I saw the food was cookies. My escort introduced me to the cookie donor and at the same time automatically removed two brown crumbs and a raisin from the white bedcover. "Mrs. Clark brings her great cookies for all our guests," the matron said. "We make them wait 'til mealtime so it won't spoil their appetite. But for Alma here it doesn't matter." She patted the bed rather lovingly and with a light sigh.

"How long has it been now?" Mrs. Clark inquired, taking another cookie from the bag and breaking off a bitesize piece to insert into the obedi-   73 ently reactive mouth. "Three years?"

"More. Close to five."

"I lose track," Mrs. Clark laughed. "But it's only a couple of years I've been feeding her cookies." She turned to me. "Once she ate *eight* of them. I don't know if it's a compliment to my baking or not." She looked into the staring eyes and started to close the bag. "That's enough today, Alma," she said. Then Mrs. Clark quickly apologized to me, opened the bag and offered me a cookie. "Take two or three—or more if you've anyone to share with."

I took one and thanked her. A few minutes later, out in the fresh air of the small community, I was aware of something crushed in my hand. I was thinking of all the butter and flour, eggs and sugar, raisins and nutmeats that go into homemade cookies. And somehow my hand had made a fist. It was ten times as big as the fist of an Indian baby reaching for dirt.

6

PROBLEMS OF HOW-TO

W_RITERS on geriatrics often preface their scholarly remarks with some general comment on long life. Perhaps they muse on the irony that increased longevity has produced new "problems of aging." Or they may note that we puzzling old folks show "less a fear of death itself than a fear of the dying process." These appear to be catch-65 comments that should have required no research beyond trying to put oneself briefly in the place of an older person. Surely we *should* fear the dying process when it has been extended intolerably, almost routinely, by every kind of pill or practice known or surmised to have the power to keep us going—going nowhere.

If we must submit to such improvements, we have a right to demand a way to avoid some of their effects. Pending the receipt of that right, we must improve our self-help methods of escape.

In the taboo-touched vocabulary of suicide, it is generally "committed," like crimes and sins and faux pas. Substitution of a better word has been difficult because of the awkward sound of less condemnatory terms: perform, accomplish, experience. Possibly we should try to popularize "accomplish" in this usage because it could encourage the actual accomplishment that so often is missed. We of the female species are truly inept suicides. Three times as many women as men attempt it; three times as many men as women make it work. Thus, the shocking failure ratio gives the ladies a reputation for flirtation with death without serious intent.

A cliché from the work-ethic days used to remind us that anything worth doing is worth doing right. This applies usefully to suicide if only because a failure often inspires well-meant gestures that make a second try more difficult. The woman who seriously means to accomplish suicide when she attempts it—and this must be true of the majority of older women—will need to bone up on how-to's.

Since the men do better, we might consider adopting their methods. Firearms top the list for American men, sleeping pills for women. Very few men use sleeping pills—perhaps one-fifth the number of women who do. But almost half as many women as men try firearms. The fact that we still show a high failure record under those circumstances may indicate that the whole question is more complicated than a mere choice of means.

76   Physical competence seems to be a factor. Our

strength, overall, is less and our mechanical aptitude (whether because of nature or conditioning) is also often less. We apparently do not shoot straight, plunge a knife competently, tie a knot or kick away a chair with true efficiency. Particularly puzzling is one study (reported in *Mental Hygiene,* July, 1969) by the research director of a suicide prevention service in Buffalo, New York, who found that even in types of suicide that should require neither strength nor mechanical aptitude, women still came in a straggling second. In cases of jumping off a high place, for example, out of 24 men who tried, 16 succeeded. But out of 27 women who tried, only 9 accomplished their goal. The 18 failures, with their catalogue of multiple mutilations, need not be described. Such a score brings up the question, certainly, if suicide *was* the women's goal. And yet jumping from a high place carries such an obvious risk that a halfway intention is hard to credit. Another study showed that even the failures of men (the reported "attempts") involved much more serious injury than the failures of women. This, in turn, brings up the further question of how many cases of women, only slightly injured in attempted suicides, were not reported at all—a fact that would make the female-male attempt rate even higher.

An interesting sidelight on jump suicides is that you can jump *out* only as far as you can jump up. Test it—you will see how limited one's scope is. A person   77 does not stand at the edge of a precipitous cliff and leap balletlike out over the chasm. You are so slightly removed from the jump-off spot, in breadth, that any small outcropping on the way down may foil (and obviously injure) you. Suicides from windows of an irregularly floored building can get caught up in awnings, be slowed by window ledges, or land on a terrace patio rather than the street below. I have a suspicion that men understand these limitations better than women. Both news stories and fiction describe male suicides who leave the window at a running jump.

One male-female difference recognized in suicide studies is the cosmetic factor. Women are historically unwilling to make themselves too unsightly even in death. A part of this reluctance, of course, may be a woman's greater sensitivity to possible shock on the part of the person who finds her. Whatever its cause, the cosmetic factor has existed from the days when the maidens of Miletus, described by Plutarch, indulged in an epidemic of hanging themselves. They were stopped when one of the wise city elders suggested that the naked bodies of the girls, adorned only with the ropes that had been their undoing, be carried through the marketplace. The epidemic, so it is said, then came to an abrupt end.

There are more sound reasons than appearance for rejecting some of the methods of suicide and carefully examining them all. Uncompleted suicide is a terrible tragedy.

78

Most means that kill will also maim and incapacitate. The physical or mental disability that may result from an attempt is particularly tragic in the young, but it also must concern the old. Part of the motivation of most elderly suicides is altruistic; even though their primary thought is to shed the burdens their own lives have become, many also want to make things a bit easier for their relatives. Thus, the unsuccessful attempt that leaves a still living but even more incapacitated and dependent person is a disaster.

Although the largest percentage of completed suicides by American men results from firearms, failure by such means also is common. A faultily aimed gun can perform a botchy frontal lobotomy and leave a living but mindless victim. A gun aimed at the heart can miss killing while damaging one of the heart chambers. A less-than-lethal dose of sleeping pills can affect mental powers by depriving brain tissue of oxygen. Carbon monoxide—a suicide route often interrupted—can inflict permanent brain damage before it kills. Poisons, unless thoroughly understood and used in the proper dosage, can cause permanent internal damage and external disfigurement —and still leave you alive. Even the history-proven means of death are not entirely dependable. Hanging is more of an art than popularly supposed, and an amateurish attempt can cause paralysis through injury of the spinal chord rather than achieve quick death.

79

Suicide is not easy. The need to plan for it secretly, to obtain the means perhaps by deception, to find the opportunity and avoid interruption—all add up to a difficult task, especially for the elderly. John Fischer (in his *Harper's* Easy Chair column mentioned in Chapter 3) said that he disliked two things about the suicide of his friend, part of whose letter referring to balance was quoted earlier here. He disliked her feeling a need to explain at all—and he was upset that she had had to build up to the act by hoarding a few pills here and there over the years. She was found in a coma and (still in a coma) lived for several days in the hospital before she died. This 80-year-old woman who had planned so well had left her affairs in meticulous order. She obviously was a sane and able person who knew her own mind —yet she could have missed. She could have been roused from the coma and forced to "live" a while longer. A pill or two less—or more, resulting in the body's rejection—might have sentenced her to still more of the life she had closed off with competent dignity. No wonder any friend would regret, as Mr. Fischer did, her necessity to rely on an unscientific dosage of hoarded pills that may have lost much of their effectiveness.

Jessamyn West, writing about her sister's suicide in *The Woman Said Yes,* makes clear the difficulty of obtaining reliable advice. The sisters had accumulated a hundred capsules on prescription by a doctor unknown to, and located far from, the doctor who attended the dying cancer patient, but Miss West needed to know a suitable dosage. She could get no hint of help from the attending doctor, even though she tried such ruses as pretending that she needed information for some of her writing and even though the doctor probably was somewhat sympathetic to the patient's wish and intention. Miss West had to guess, also, at the probable length of the coma that would precede death, because she must make arrangements for her sister to be undisturbed for a safe period of time and to avoid, at all costs, hospitalization with its inevitable interfering and "life-saving" techniques. In the end, the suicide was accomplished after a 24-hour coma. Its completion had required the careful planning and firm will of two highly intelligent women who did not underestimate their need for self-reliance at the crucial time.

Advance planning must include a continuing awareness of one's own system and reactions. Get into the habit of asking your doctor questions about any drug prescribed for you. Seek—and note down —any information about "safe" limits and how much they can be stretched. Observe your own reactions, especially if adverse, to any pain-killers or soporifics. If nausea accompanies a pain-killing dosage of a prescription drug, you don't have to be an expert to know your body probably would reject an overdose.

Learn about injections—perhaps by taking a first-

81

aid course or by a friendly chat with a diabetic friend who takes daily insulin. Keep your mind open to receive and store enough common-sense medical information to prevent you from taking a faulty and futile step.

When you read a news story about a suicide or "mercy killing," watch for details and make them a subject of discussion with friends who might have expertise in the area. There was a famous case some years ago of a doctor on trial for ending a patient's tortured life by injecting air—to make an "air bubble" in a vein. This sounded remarkably simple and possibly useful. I, presumably along with millions of others, held onto this scrap of information as though it would one day come in handy. In due time, however, I read Lael Tucker Wertenbaker's impressive account of her husband's difficult suicide (*Death of a Man*), which finally was achieved (in a case of advanced cancer) only through morphine injections plus bloodletting. In this book, Mr. Wertenbaker passes most of one pain-wracked day "playing the bubbles game" in an effort to find the release that had sounded so available. But it was not easy, nor even possible, and the Wertenbakers decided the air bubble must be reserved for doctors.

Dr. Paul Lafargue (son-in-law of Karl Marx), who chose the age of 70 for his death and carried it out in a double suicide along with his wife, left a note detailing the means: "I have fixed the moment for my departure from life and I have prepared the method of executing my project: a hypodermic injection of hydrocyanic acid . . ." He was a doctor, although not a practicing one.

The traditional means of suicide favored by women before sleeping-pill days depended very much on availability. Drowning was common until fairly recent times. Bodies of water generally were available, with most cities built on shorelines or along rivers. Indian women often jumped into wells, and this still is a fairly common village means of suicide in India. In Japan, the ancient ritual decreed a knife-cut at the throat for women (opposed to the ritualized de-boweling of men) and this practice still is followed by some.

The advent of household gas brought a ready means for female suicides, although now the increased use of natural gas in the U.S. has made this method impractical without undue risk to others. Natural gas, unlike coal gas, is nonpoisonous. It can kill only by replacing oxygen to cause suffocation, or through the damage done by an explosion of the accumulated gas. Distributors of natural gas in the U.S. commonly use an additive to call attention to the presence of leaking (odorless) gas. In Great Britain, gas has until recently been the top choice for suicides, with 561 out of 1000 suicides ascribed to gas in 1959 and 322 out of 1000 as late as 1965 (when sleeping pills took over first place with 486

83

in 1000). North Sea resources now are supplying natural gas, and by mid-1977 conversion to natural gas had been accomplished in 98% of English households.

Britain's effective gun control puts suicide by fire-arms near the bottom of the list there. Hanging, for both men and women and in most countries, continues to be the solution for many.

In discussing ways and means, we probably should take a quick look at some of the theories about suicide. Many of these do not apply to the elderly because no real search for motive and little theorizing about relative pressures, and so on, is required to find the likely reason for the action. Nevertheless, one aspect of suicide theory must concern us: are we actually capable of it?

Many psychologists and psychiatrists agree that in-turned aggression is an important factor in suicide and some have declared flatly that no one kills herself or himself without wishing to kill another. They also point out that wishing to kill another, or at least wishing another dead, is a common if not universal feeling. Most old people must have had these wishes, no matter how dormant or half-forgotten. They may be evident as well, of course—we may wish more or less everyone but our suffering selves to be dead on occasion, and we may scatter unaimed hostility in all directions even after our close friends or relatives—common targets—are gone. Assuming, then, this necessary component of aggression, are we capable of in-turning it?

Dr. Karl Menninger has reasoned that three elements are required for suicide:

The wish to kill (aggression)
The wish to be killed (punishment)
The wish to die, to be dead (death instinct)

If any of the three is absent, Dr. Menninger concluded, the suicide usually will not be completed. Further research into these three elements (by E. S. Shneidman and N. L. Farberow in the 1950s) based on analysis of suicide notes indicated that wishes to kill and be killed decrease with age, while the wish to die increases.

Taking the elements in reverse order, one might surmise that (as the study mentioned above indicates) most of the elderly who consider suicide sincerely wish to be dead. The life-clinging elderly, of whom there are many, probably do not even think of suicide. Medical personnel tell many stories of persons who, even though in extreme pain and experiencing prolonged suffering, show no sign of wishing to weaken their hold on life. Their attitude often surprises doctors and nurses.

The wish to be killed is a large factor in the "indirect" suicides that confuse statistics. When a person, old or young, steps in front of a fast-moving car as he or she leaves the curb it may be an accident. Or 85 it may be suicide. Accidents in motor cars, especially where the driver is the only occupant, are assumed to be a mixture of "pure" accident, unconscious suicide (or subintentional death, in the more expert language of professionals), deliberate suicide, et cetera. Excessive use of alcohol and other drugs often is seen as "chronic suicide." The use of cigarettes also comes into that category now that mortality figures traceable to heavy smoking are beginning to be known. Our rejection of gun control laws may be a manifestation of the death wish. The means of "indirect" suicide are numerous, and many appear to be closely associated with the wish to be killed.

So we might reason that the elderly person contemplating suicide can qualify under Dr. Menninger's second and third points. The largest question is likely to be number one—does she or he wish to kill? Or, wishing to kill, is the wish strong enough to assure the successful carrying out of the act?

To many individuals, this may be the most important point in the "how-to's" of suicide. No matter what the specific means, or how thorough the background planning, something may trip us up at the crucial moment. A lot of that something may be nothing more than our long conditioning to the idea of sin and crime and shame, but it is no less real. Its existence is a primary reason for talking about suicide and for promoting a group attitude that can lend support to the lonely individual who, while not doubting her resolve, does fear her inability. For some people, the suicide pact or the comfort of a bit of aiding and abetting are necessary propellants for reluctant in-turned aggression.

An interesting and possibly helpful sidelight in arriving at our own attitude involves the suicide rate among doctors and psychiatrists. That rate is significantly higher than in the general population—reportedly three to five times as high for physicians and six to ten times for psychiatrists. Doctors, of course, have the knowledge and the means readily available if and when they decide on suicide. The figures also suggest that our medical caretakers may not be as firmly against self-destruction as their public attitudes often indicate. Their greater familiarity with both birth and death also may make the choice and the act of suicide a simpler thing for them. Nevertheless, medical experts appear to have a taboo-type attitude toward their suicides. The *Journal of the American Medical Association* did not list any deaths as suicides until the 1960s—a slashed wrist was termed hemorrhage, strangling was asphyxiation, and so on.

The medical-world suicide rates tell us, too, to aim for self-reliance within possible bounds. Our doctors and psychiatrists have their own problems from which they, no less than we, look for a way out.

Our social and medical "establishment" appears determined to close as many of those ways as possible. There was a time when a determined old person could simply stop taking nourishment—an era, one suspects, when the sight of a threatening array of today's tubes and bottles hitched up to a failing body would have scared a few people to death. The "migratory" suicides, noted with yet another new tag, take people from place to place looking for relief from pain or loneliness or from general *anomie*, and these contribute to the high suicide rates in California and Florida. But there is no place to migrate where we can avoid penicillin for pneumonia or be sure that the newspaper boy won't notify the good-works people that something is amiss in a house or apartment where a peaceful coma is just getting nicely under way.

We are beleaguered. Perhaps this is a good thing if it can arouse in us the necessary aggression to qualify for the one-two-three of successful suicide. We will need a certain degree of toughness. Curious about hemlock, I looked it up in the encyclopedia only to find that the poisonous varieties promote anything but an easy death. Is the hemlock of Attica extinct, or are we so used to the easy life that we can contemplate no deliberately induced pain, however brief? Someone told me that even cyanide "gives you a bad few seconds." The obvious answer is, "Yes, but it may eliminate a bad few years." And the obvious answer to *that* is, "Of course. But you can't be sure of that. Bad years sneak up on you."

Although these bad years sneak up, and while we await with caution the signs of their coming, we can discuss suicide so as to feel both more accepting and more capable. What we need, and should ask for on all possible occasions, is an available and reliable dosage, the legal right to use it and the legal right to have help in obtaining or taking it. Bizarre and innovative suicides happen, but they are tricky and unreliable and tend to make suicide seem exhibition-istic rather than practical. We want common sense methods that can be used in a common-sense way.

Many women have a special field of knowledge that they could share reassuringly with the untu-tored. Group discussions of suicide could welcome chemists, medical personnel, pharmacists, publicists, lawyers, historians, herbalists and anyone else—fe-male or male, young or old—with a good reliable word for a good self-controlled death.

There is interesting lore in the annals of suicide and plenty of room for more investigation into both its heavy and light sides. Room to prove that there *are* two sides, or many. There are fads in suicide—from the maids of Miletus to the veritable "run" on a Japanese mountain in the 1930s. This run was one of the more strenuous fads. It began after a school-girl threw herself into the thousand-foot crater of Mt. Mihara on Oshima Island, fifty miles southwest of Tokyo, and did not end until almost a hundred people had followed the girl's lead and hundreds 89 more were forcibly deterred. The record catch of the volcano was six young men in one Sunday afternoon.

A remarkable thing about the Mt. Mihara suicides was the difficulty of it all. According to a London *Daily Mail* reporter who took the trip, it started with a five-hour steamer ride from Tokyo, a long trek through "deep green lanes like those of Devonshire" to the foot of the mountain, then a climb through a "forest of azalea and camellia bushes, gleaming with voluptuous flowers"—then the rough part began. This involved a camel-back ride across a "desert of lava," then a pony-back climb up the steep ascent and, finally, one must "stumble half a mile over sharp-edged lava boulders to the crater's edge." Possibly, after all this, the way back seemed at least as bad as the way onward into the crater.

The devotees of Mt. Mihara were mostly young, and they had to be vigorous to get into position. The how-to means they chose really are irrelevant for aging Americans, but this small "epidemic" illustrates something of the variety found in a subject we too seldom discuss. Japanese suicides alone—their ritual and the attitudes they reinforced through many generations—could supply a wealth of study material for a consciousness-raising course on suicide.

Any how-to discussion must include the question of how not to harm others in doing away with our-

90

selves. With modern apartment living, urban and suburban crowding, the flimsiness of walls and the carelessness of both adults and children, it is not easy to contain the damage that may result from gases, fires and misfirings—literal or figurative.

Carbon monoxide willfully released by a suicide from the exhaust of a running motor into a closed basement garage of a two-family house can kill or incapacitate all the residents. Careless storage of some poisonous substance, only a small amount of which was consumed by a suicide, can be a time-bomb for trouble. (A posthumous vote of thanks was due to the old man who left this simple note: "Don't worry about me—get rid of that weed killer under the sink.") Attempted head-in-the-oven suicides, in any kind of multiple-dwelling structure, risk fire and explosion affecting a wide area. The liberal use of the gas method by English suicides has resulted in less peripheral damage than might be expected because of the cut-off feature of pay-as-you-go devices. A shilling-in-the-meter system, although presumably not designed for suicides, must nevertheless have saved the conscientious exiter some last minute worries. But this device is becoming obsolete and never was widely available to U.S. suicides. Jumping off a high place is one of the earliest methods of suicide, and one of the safest for the primitive societies of the wide open spaces. Jumping from a high floor of an urban skyscraper remains sure-fire for the jumper but imposes a burden of risk for ground-level pedestrians.

The legal term "transferred malice" is used in connection with the injuring of another person by one attempting suicide. This damage often is done to someone who tries to intervene—an unwelcome lifesaver. And in freak accidents, a bullet deflected from its intended target has been known to kill a stranger at some distance.

The elderly suicide has no "malice" to spare. We need to channel it to fulfill our quota of in-turned aggression and can afford to be meticulously careful about confining our lethal efforts to ourselves. Because a part of our motivation may be the altruistic wish to make life easier for others, we will be careful not to make our finale a fiasco.

7

FRINGE BENEFITS

AFTER you have decided that suicide
ought to be legal, isn't a sin, and that you have some
knowledge of how to do it, a big barrier still looms.
Your loved ones.

You have heard and read throughout your life
that suicide brings a flood of woe to those left behind. People lower their voices when speaking of it
and whisper rumors. "Going *that* way—so hard for
the family." Or, "Yes, I hear there was no note, but
he was always the thoughtless one—poor so-and-so"
(so-and-so being the widow or orphan, son or
daughter or distant cousin). Or, "They say it runs in
the family—such a burden." Much clicking of
tongues.

One is left with the impression that the survivors
will have a lot of "living down" to do before their
reputations as members-in-good-standing of our sui-
cide-taboo society are clear again.

Again, you have a right to ask: what is this all
about? How did it start?

It started with the age-old fear of ghosts. It was perpetuated through religion and law. We know well enough how it started. The only mystery is how and why we allow it to persist.

When an elderly person dies most people can see some advantages for the survivors. "George'll be able to travel now—he was tied down by his mother's illness." Or "I hear the house goes to the granddaughter—her kids will finally have a yard to play in."

People look on the bright side after the funeral. That is, if it is a "natural" death, a respectable death. "Yes, she just slipped away in her sleep. Such a blessing—"

But if someone slipped her a pill so she could lengthen and deepen her sleep—the blessing is transformed into bad news.

The method of death, in itself, cannot change the facts of life for the living. Only the *attitude* toward that method can, and often does, make the episode tragic. The what-will-people-think consideration (because we know all too well what they will think) may give us pause.

If we do not want our intention foiled by a mere attitude, we can take the forethought to change that attitude, both among our close friends and relatives and also in general. We can talk about suicide and refuse to participate in gossipy cover-up attitudes. We can be critical of hypocritical opinions that ig-

94

nore facts. We can accent the positive by pointing out and publicizing the good side of any suicide case with which we are familiar. And certainly, in our own planning, we can prepare to relieve, in advance, the kind of burden that may be imposed by uncertainty (i.e., nothing anyone else did is causing this—it's my long-chosen way out) and make our going a useful event in any possible way. There *are* fringe benefits for others in many elderly common-sense suicides. We must only recognize and make the most of them.

"I think most adults can understand old-age suicide," a friend suggested. "But it would be hard to explain to kids."

This difficulty seems exaggerated, especially in light of all the other things that must be hard to explain to kids these days—such as why they have to be sent to bed before the TV programs explode in a blood-bath of violence for the amusement of their elders or the lines waiting to buy tickets for the X-rated movie at the neighborhood theatre. Old people seem much older to kids than they do to adults—and old people *do* die in various ways. If suicide is presented as one of those ways, it will be accepted as one of the ways.

A man in his fifties recalls the first suicide he ever heard of. It was the father of a friend and it occurred during the bank-failure epidemic of the depression. The boys were six or seven, perhaps, and the bank-

95

er-father of the friend went home to lunch one day, climbed the stairs to the bathroom and shot himself in the head. "I just assumed bankers commit suicide," the man says now. "I can't remember feeling anything in particular about it. Maybe I was glad my dad wasn't a banker—but I don't remember that, I'm just tagging it on now." He laughed. "Funny— I never really got over that first impression. When I need to speak to an officer of my bank—which is rarely—I sometimes wonder if he's still around. This first suicide made bankers somehow expendable."

It would be tempting to extrapolate too much comfort from this simple tale: make old-age suicide acceptable to one generation of children and the attitude is reversed. First thing you know, kids will be wondering not why we do, but why we *don't.* Of course it is not that easy, but it may be much easier than anyone would have thought a decade or two ago. Attitudes toward almost everything have changed drastically; why not toward suicide?

Among the young, such attitudes may have changed more than we recognize. A part of the change is their own increased acceptance of suicide —unfortunately for themselves rather than for the old. The suicide rate in the U.S. (but not in the U.S. alone) has been increasing more rapidly in the under-24 age group than in the over-65. There is a recognizable, unarguable difference between planned suicides among the elderly and the impul-

sive act of a young person who may be supersensi-
tive, temporarily depressed or simply lacking the
maturity to be slightly objective about her or his
actual circumstances.

Much is made of the statistical fact that suicide
now is the second cause of death (next to accidents)
among American youth. This is not as alarming as it
sounds, because there are almost no unconquered
diseases that affect children and once accounted for
the low life-expectancy figures. Young people today
hardly ever die "naturally"; they do die in large
numbers by accident, mainly automobile accident.
And the second cause (a lagging second) is, indeed,
suicide. If some of the car accidents also are assumed
to be suicide, the numbers are adequate for alarm.
Further, if abuse of alcohol and other drugs is accepted as "chronic" suicide, things look even worse.

Can we, as elderly suicides, have any effect on the
young people who, like us and yet terribly *un*like us,
are looking for an exit?

The answer might be a cautious yes. If we are able
to break the taboo, get the subject of suicide out into
the open, and popularize it (both in word and in
fact) as the logical, the "right" and available, choice
for the failing and ailing old, some of the impulsive
young might be turned off by the whole picture. The
old are always accused, often correctly, of imitating
the young. But this seldom works in the opposite
direction. Young people are not famous imitators of

97

the old once they get beyond the I-want-to-be-a-fireman-when-I-grow-up stage.

On the practical level, a linking of suicide prevention and suicide facilitation, probably through existing or similar suicide prevention centers, could make the contrast between the planned and impulsive types more visible. It could also provide a forum for an interchange of views between the planners and the impulsives, if this would be useful. One can imagine that an elderly person planning a rational suicide would be willing to take "time out" to talk with a younger person who showed suicidal tendencies. Whether or not such talks would be beneficial is a decision for members of the staff familiar with each individual situation. In specific cases it seems possible that a younger person would have some new things to think about after a chat with the elder. Additional fall-out would include the research possibilities implied in a situation where two very different kinds of people, sharing little except a tendency to exchange life for death, meet on a safe and neutral ground in a protected atmosphere.

I once heard an old man express disdain for a young relative who had attempted suicide. "He was educated in mathematics," the old man said, "but he won't see the odds of the gamble. Now if *I* was to gamble on the Hereafter it would make sense— what have I got to lose? A young fellow like that has a Herenow. He shouldn't be taking a chance on a Hereafter."

Such an opinion, expressed in a group discussion among young and old at a suicide center might stimulate useful get-it-off-your-chest admissions, as might the reminiscences of the expendable-banker man. Think about your own first knowledge of suicide (if you can recall it); analyze how it might fit into group discussion. Try to decide whether it would be useful and attempt to guess what responses it would call forth from the young. And if you get too curious, try it out on any young friends you may have. It's an interesting experiment.

Jacques Choron, who has worked with suicide prevention both at an urban (Los Angeles) center and on a national level through the National Institute of Mental Health, points out in his book *Suicide* that there are widespread misconceptions about the activity of suicide prevention centers. He states that "there is no conflict between suicide prevention and the position that suicide is an inherent right of each individual." Such centers provide an opportunity— a reply to the "cry for help" *if* such a reply is wanted or useful. The centers do not force their services on anyone. And Mr. Choron, in his discussion of euthanatic suicides, suggests that once the principle of such suicide is accepted, the supplying of means to any individual "does not exclude giving the candidates the opportunity to avail themselves of the services of suicide prevention centers before making the final decision."

One need go only a little beyond this suggestion   99

to visualize a time when obtaining the means for efficient suicide by an elderly person might itself be a function of similar centers. Specialists in suicide who have encountered thousands of persons in the centers would seem to be the best qualified to judge the state of mind of an elderly intended suicide or to evaluate prerecorded intentions in cases of mental incapacity.

Such a function, again, would help to draw a distinct line between the types of suicide. It should also make the centers themselves better known and better supported. Every family has its old people, many of whom will find it big news and good news to learn —soon, we can hope—that legal suicide, complete with counseling and help, is available. The suicide prevention centers now number more than 200 in the U.S. and are increasing, although not as fast as the need. If the elderly should come within their specific purview, more and better centers would be established.

The recording of a suicide intention, whether at such centers or elsewhere, under whatever legal provisions, also can provide an important fringe benefit for the suicide's family or close friends. Many suicide cases are now surrounded by mystery as to real motive and intent. Circumstances may combine to make an actual suicide look like a malicious deed; or a malicious deed— a homicide—may appear to be simple suicide.

Undoubtedly there are occasional miscarriages of justice—and these tend to have a burdensome effect on the survivors no matter how peacefully the suicide has disappeared from the scene. When there is provision to prerecord one's intention to accomplish suicide under more or less specific conditions, this air of mystery will be dispelled. In some cases, widespread prerecording of an intention might even be an aid to justice. If a person who appears to be a suicide has not recorded the intention but is the type who normally would have taken advantage of this aspect of "putting things in order," then the authorities may be alerted to carry out a more thorough investigation than otherwise would have been called for.

The availability of legal suicide and its frequent use by senior citizens should carry enormous benefits for fellow seniors who will end their days in an institution but do not choose to limit those days by any act of their own. This number will include, of course, those many pathetic residents no longer capable of decisions and whose relatives do not feel qualified or entitled to make a decision for them. If every nursing home, whether nonprofit or all-for-profit, had to compete with painless and peaceful death to keep its residents, who can doubt that some changes would be made?

Today's tolerance for substandard institutions is based on a no-alternative, last-resort demand. Unscrupulous or incompetent operators often are not exposed because their services—vicious as these services may be—are necessary.

A woman who has done extensive volunteer work in an urban nursing home says she will time her taking of the fatal pill to the ride to the nursing home. "I want to get there just in time for them to call the undertaker," she said. "Maybe that will wake a few people up."

Possibly a golden-age option for suicide, exercised liberally, would also affect the direction of research. Although much of the gerontological research presumably is aimed at "quality of life," the most obvious results appear (to the aging layman) to be prolongation. If this prolongation is a result of general medical research—against specific diseases, nutritional studies, and so on—then the interrelation between fields of research may be out of balance. Freedom of research cannot and should not be curtailed, but the subjects of the research (who are "aging mice" in many experiments but also "aging people" in real life) should have the open option to say ENOUGH.

When quality-of-life catches up to mere quantity, more individuals may choose to renew their suicide option or even let it lapse. Right now, however, this option is needed. When it is available, its use will send a message to the research labs.

102   A fringe benefit we ourselves can bring about is

the donation of useful vital organs for transplant. A British attorney, Mary Barrington, is quoted as saying, "A patient near the end of his life who arranged his death so as, for example, to permit an immediate transfer of a vital organ to a younger person, might well feel that he was converting his death into a creative act instead of waiting passively to be suppressed."

There also are nonmedical possibilities for allowing our passing to be a creative act. A woman who lived alone in a large house in an urban area watched her neighborhood change and most of the old residents die or move away to be replaced by families of another culture. She took an interest in the changes, while she was able, and then set about the task of making a legal transfer of her property, upon her death, to the parents of a little girl among the newcomers who had become her friend. The woman was in failing health, but not acutely ill. Her attorney did not anticipate her death within one week after all the papers were in order. No one expected it quite so soon, for it was an efficiently achieved suicide. And a "creative act" at the same time.

One of the saddest aspects of many suicides is the mystery that surrounds the mood of the person who chose to give up life. What did Virginia Woolf feel and think when she waded into the river with her pockets heavy with stones? What dark mood impelled Sylvia Plath to turn on the gas in the kitchen —risking the lives of her children in an upstairs room? The survivors may be tormented by these questions for years, and an answer cannot come.

The suicide of an elderly person must raise fewer questions, but that is not to say it raises none at all. A daughter who has allowed her mother to remain alone in the family home, despite her likely inability to manage well there, will always wonder if the toxic household helpers and the mother's medicines— found jumbled together in confusion on the kitchen counter—really were mixed up by accident or desperate design. Another daughter who insisted on moving her mother out of the old home, only to lose her to an overdose of sleeping pills a few months later, will ask herself why she forced the change. Wherever or however the suicide occurs, someone will be questioning the circumstances, the reasons, the mood.

An unusually happy case of a clue to a mood was related to me by a friend. "I hadn't seen my cousin for several years," she told me, "and the shock of seeing how she'd aged, how very ill she looked, was a big one. But she was as bright and talkative as ever, as quick with her witty remarks. In half an hour I was hardly conscious of her appearance. She liked to shop and had good taste about clothes and a lot of enthusiasm about them. Somehow the subject came up after lunch and she took me into the bedroom to

slide open the closet doors and show me some purchase she was proud of. I think it was a dress for
some special occasion. Hanging right next to it was
a youthful denim jumpsuit with white daisies embroidered on the yoke. She half tried to hide it—
then laughed at herself and took it off the rod to
show me. 'I like it, and it's quite unsuitable to my
age or figure,' she said. 'I suppose I'll never wear it.'
And then, before I could comment, she said, 'No,
I *will* wear it. I'll wake up some morning feeling full
of daring and I'll wear my daisied denim. Why not?'
We laughed together.

"I didn't see her again. Only a few weeks later we
got word that she'd drowned at a lake about thirty
miles from her home. It was fairly obviously a suicide. We learned then, too, that she was as ill as she
had looked and probably in much more pain than
she had allowed to show. But the most significant
thing I learned from the details of her death was that
she was wearing a denim jumpsuit. I knew then that
she had not gone drearily. She had awakened 'full
of daring' and ready to take her fate into her own
capable hands. I felt I had a precious insight into her
final mood and I was glad I could share it with her
son and daughter."

When suicide is legal, acceptable, ethical—okay
in all possible ways—we the aging should be relieved of many varieties of fear and anxiety. We can
set our affairs in order if we're the tidy type, go on   105

a spending spree if we're frivolous and have the means, dump all our burdensome decisions on our "committee of the person" and proceed relatively carefree to our self-appointed final hour.

This, you may say, is a totally selfish view. It is not a fringe benefit.

True. But old people are notoriously cantankerous and difficult at times. Allow us to shed some of our worst fears of pain and disability, of isolation and loneliness, of loss of our functions, loss of our minds, loss of any shred of dignity. Let us shed those and we might be much, much easier to live with while we decide to live. That *is* a fringe benefit.

8

OUR SOCIETY

WE commonly hear some of the ill treatment of the elderly blamed on the fact that "our
society" is mad about youth and dangerously tilted
pro-youth in all its attitudes. I'm not sure how true
this is. If it *is* true, is it all bad?

Entering a hotel meeting-room along with a large
number of AARP (American Association of Retired
Persons) members to hear about AARP travel plans,
one of the women said to the man with her, "Look
over this crowd. Old people just don't look old any
more. They take care of themselves."

Undoubtedly "this crowd" would have looked
old to young people. But our mutual view, among
ourselves, probably was that we didn't look all that
old. We didn't resemble the "old folks" we remembered from our own youth. Or, grey-haired and
dentured as we might be, we didn't look as old as
the 96-year-old we had visited in hospital recently.
Feeling ourselves less than frightfully old, we do, as
the woman said, take care of ourselves.　107

And yet this taking care, to some extent, is the thing that is criticized as the madness of our youth culture. Small elderly women who fit into the same dress as their granddaughters may sometimes buy such a dress. We purchase cosmetics as if we were young enough to care how we look. We have our hair touched up or go to exercise classes to get rid of bulges. We may take a course in art appreciation, learn enough about accounting to improve our income-tax situation, or study Spanish in order to meet halfway the Guatamalan girl who comes in for weekly cleaning. Yes—we even think we're young enough to learn things.

The fact that we stay in shape longer may be merely part of the fact that we live longer. Our society is a society that has added so many years to life that the classical ages of man, or woman, have become distorted. We have added years enough for a whole "age"—and if we choose to use it at the youthful end of the scale rather than prolonging the old-age bit, why not? It seems unfair to blame "our society" for a choice that is not only our own to a fair extent but one that also makes sense.

The argument that we have become so youth-oriented that we cannot stand the sight of our old-sters—and thus that we send them off to storage in nursing homes—appears overharsh in its implied indictment of anyone under nursing-home age and degree of debility. Our pursuit of youth surely must have kept many older people *out* of nursing homes by prolonging their period of self-reliance and competence.

Independence, for so long as we can take it, is a good thing. It helps keep the elderly in shape, both mentally and physically, to cope with their needs. The loss of independence, and the beginning of having to depend on someone else, can initiate a quick decline into extensive or total dependence. We live longer and longer; we live part of those years more competently than in the past; we still outlive that competence and, bolstered up by endless medicines and fortifiers and extraordinary attention, large numbers of us still end up in unattractive circumstances. If we enter the period of incompetence a little later, and if we attain the right to leave it at will or on a pre-planned schedule, we probably will have made the best possible job of this burden of added years.

There is much nostalgia about the extended family and the delightful old granny by the fire, worshipped by all. These stories are mostly myth. Our ancestors rarely lived long enough to become remembered fixtures by the fire; the few "characters" recalled in tale-telling and some who were set down in fiction were exceptions to a rule of timely demise. And anyone who can remember nursing an aging relative through a winter illness when there was no central heating, no running water, no sewer, no "disposable" anything—and of course no miracle medicines—is unlikely to be sentimental about the way it "used to be" for the old folks. It used to be long on pain and short on cures. It was a period when opium and morphine were, of necessity, dispensed as freely as aspirin is today.

An old man wheeling himself through a nursing-home corridor apparently detected a that's-a-bad-odor expression on a young woman's face while she waited for the elevator. "Don't be turning up your nose, Miss," he said, pulling to a stop. "You've smelled no bad smell 'til you know gangrene in a sod house. Never heard of anything like that, huh? Well, it happened to my grandfather. I was only a lad. I'll never forget that stench." He shook his head. " 'Course he died," the old man added, wheeling off. "Buried his leg that winter and him in the spring."

"What's a sod house?" the girl said to no one in particular, looking a little stunned. The elevator came and no one tried to tell her. But the old man's words had conjured up a terrible picture. The extended family in a tiny sod house, dealing with a mortal infection (requiring amputation) plus the normal crises of pioneer life. It is not the stuff for a frontier days TV romance. But it probably was quite common. A doctor who addressed a symposium on the elderly last year declared that our country "was founded on neglect of the elderly" and cited the way

110

the young went west in pioneer days leaving their elderly behind. Perhaps it was neglect, but it must have worked out to be a mercy in many instances too. Life on the frontier was not ideal for the old folks.

Nor is it ideal in any of the "other societies" we sometimes hear cited in contrast to our own. Most other cultures have a smaller proportion of old than do we; they handle their problems less extravagantly and leave more of the responsibility to the family. To assume from this that the family care is always loving, gentle and rewarding is nonsense. The aging Indian woman is cared for in her extended family situation not by a daughter but by one or more of the daughters-in-law. Those girls who came into the household as young brides and took orders from the senior woman down through the years *may* be loving and patient but more likely are not. Now that the tables are turned, they may repay the old woman with much of the abuse she laid on them. Mother-in-law problems exist around the globe. They are the subject of many jokes in the West; they are too serious for jokes in the East.

Elderly Japanese, especially in rural areas, used to retain a position of respect, usually in the household of the eldest son. With rapid industrialization, many of the old now are left in the countryside, unable to work effectively, while the younger members of the household go to the cities for industrial jobs. Sui- 111 cides among these elderly Japanese are very common.

In the agricultural societies of Asia and Africa, where the sustenance of millions of people may depend on whims of weather, the society can have few scruples about feeding its productive members first. In China the old are kept busy looking after the toddlers—a useful task that allows both parents to put in a day's work, but an arrangement hardly adaptable to advanced industrialization. In the USSR extended family living is forced by the housing shortage and is the cause of much domestic tension.

Reverence for old age, historically, stemmed in part from superstition and in part from practicality. Fear of ghosts, awe of ancestors and their power— these, more than any family affection, shaped the respectful attitude of the young to those elders who formed a bridge to the unknown ghost world. In the days of few elders, those few also were the repository of much of the tribe's or clan's knowledge. They may have had skills to pass on. Their remembrance of events and of the tales of their own elders provided a comforting continuity. They were prized for a discernible value.

Today we take our history from book or film, our skills from vocational training rather than from an elder craftsman. Both the rarity and the usefulness of the elder have become obsolete. We are increas-

112

ingly overstocked with elders, and an aspect of the age shift in our population is a growth in suicides. This is occurring, however, not merely in "our" society. It happens to a lesser degree in ours than in many others.

So far we haven't talked much about suicide rates. The suicide statistics are, at best, incomplete and controversial. Even on a national scale, criteria for reported suicides differ from state to state. Some small towns may never come up with one suicide— but half an hour with the town gossip would produce the names of several. On an international scale, tremendous differences are involved. The World Health Organization recognizes this fact and is attempting to fashion a set of acceptable rules for suicide reporting, but accurate statistics that can be compared usefully across national borders are a thing of the future. Meanwhile, and bearing in mind the many differences of definition, evaluation, and national and personal prejudice that must affect the reporting, we still can get some indication of the situation.

The rates refer to the number of suicides per annum for every 100,000 of population. Taking the U.S. population at 215 million, our approximate 27,000 suicides in 1975 would give a rate of about 12.6. The actual statistics, in the U.S. and in most reporting countries, are split up to reflect sex, age group, race, et cetera. The male rate, as we have

noted before, far outstrips the female rate in the
U.S. and in most places (actually everywhere, except
for certain age groups in Japan where suicide is the
largest cause of death for women in the 20 to 29 age
group). The rate for whites also is far higher than for
nonwhites. And this is a good place to mention a few
of the peripheral influences affecting rates. In recent
years both the female rate and the nonwhite rate in
the U.S. have been on the rise. No one is sure
whether there is an actual increase or whether reporting patterns have changed. There is some belief
that suicides among blacks are now more conscien-
tiously reported than they were a decade ago and
also that fewer (usually male) coroners hesitate to
pronounce a woman a suicide in cases where once
they would have "protected her good name." On
the other hand, some psychologists believe that
while no real increase in suicide can be ascribed to
the women's liberation movement, both women and
blacks in the U.S. have been subjected to strains
imposed by a rapidly changing status.

Back to the rates. Meaningful or not, they are
surprisingly consistent down through the years.
Hungary (with a rate of 36.9 in 1972) heads the list;
Hungary headed the list in 1897 as well as today and
all through the years of tremendous political
change. Denmark (24.7) and Austria (23.3) usually
vie for second place, although in the 1972 figures
Czechoslovakia (24.2) and East Germany (30.5)

were higher. Many communist countries, including both the USSR and China, do not participate in the WHO study, and some East European nations do not consistently report. Thus, the high East German figure cannot be compared with other years, although it offers a comparison to West Germany (21.2) for the same year. Ireland, with a 2.3 rate in 1972, maintained her usual low place on the scale (often credited to Catholicism, which must be one of the factors, although high ranking Austria also is heavily Catholic).

Scandinavia is the perennial puzzler to suicide experts. Denmark's high rates, along with Finland's 21.7 and Sweden's 20.4, are set off against Norway with only 8.1. These are 1972 figures (when our U.S. rate was 11.7), but they are typical of the Scandinavian pattern. The wide discrepancy provides endless opportunities for research and a number of conflicting theories. We can learn, for instance, that the long dark winter in Finland brings the family into close togetherness—with a spate of suicides bursting out in the spring along with the sun. But Denmark's weather is cited less than the Danish upbringing of children who, we are told, are disciplined through guilt: "look how unhappy you are making mummy"—and who thus learn to impose suffering in the same way. Their suicides, under this theory, punish the living. Others attribute the high Danish rate to an historical, if inexplicable, melancholy. Economically conservative theorizers like to tie the high Scandinavian rates to the deleterious effects of too much welfare. And one U.S. suicide expert, who did on-location research in all the Scandinavian countries, writes rather wryly of the difficulty of approaching Norwegians in an effort to learn why more of them did not do themselves in.

Japan, where the *attitude* toward suicide differs from the rest of the world more than the rate, had a 17.0 rate in 1972. This was almost identical to the Sri Lanka rate, although the two Asian societies could hardly be more different. One way in which the Japanese rates relate to our own is the great increase of suicide among young people. Rapid changes in Japanese society have broken traditional patterns for both young and old and for the relations between them. Japanese elders may choose suicide when they feel abandoned by their offspring or when they feel they may become a burden on the younger family members. Then the children in turn may choose the same way out if they are oppressed by guilt. Elderly Japanese women (75 and up) have the highest suicide rate in the world, with many of the acts blamed on daughter-in-law conflict.

Japanese psychiatrist Takeyama explains that the traditional obedience of Japanese youth remains a basic unconscious influence that is in sharp conflict with their conscious striving to adjust to modern western ways. This conflict increases with the degree

116

of education and 40% of Japanese students are said
to have contemplated suicide at least once. Our U.S.
newspapers report the high figures on their completed suicides every year at exam time. Dr.
Takeyama adds, "Juvenile delinquents rarely consider it, because they take out their frustrations in
criminal acts against society." This fact, too, may
relate to our U.S. problems.

The relation between suicide and other forms of
violence (or suicide by other names if one goes for
the broadest definitions) is evident. Suicide in war-
time is traditionally low (but war itself has been
called "mass suicide"). The assumption is that the
war atmosphere allows other outlets for aggression
and ties the alienated individual into some group—
if only "our side" against the enemy. There appears,
also, to be a so-far unidentified relation between
suicide and homicide rates. In the U.S., our suicide
rates traditionally have been about one and one-half
times the homicide rate. The gap is narrowing somewhat, but not significantly enough to bear analysis.
Some researchers point to a possible balancing out
—where suicide is high (as in Denmark), homicide
may be low (as happens to be the case with Denmark). But no widely reliable pattern of this kind
has been demonstrated. It obviously is temptingly
simple to see an X-mass of violence for a given
society and then to analyze how it is distributed, but
the approach has not yielded impressive results.   117

Without having any opinion on the matter, however, one can guess that it may be preferable to live in a society where there is more suicide than homicide—wouldn't you rather have a suicide than a murder on your block?

While we're on this rather primitive subject, a quick look at the primitive societies yields a few more puzzling facts about the role of the elderly and their use of suicide. Leo W. Simmons in his *Primitive Society* states that out of seventeen tribes on which data could be gathered, suicide by the elderly was frequent in eleven tribes, rare in four and almost nonexistent in two. Old age itself was rare enough, and neglect and abandonment were not uncommon. Accusations of witchcraft might justify segregation or ill-treatment of the old. A researcher who compared motivations for suicide (in general, including the elderly) among primitive groups found "quarrels with kin" came second only to physical distress from illness or injury among some tribes. A neighboring tribe, however, might put family quarrels low on the list and accent personal integrity. Suicide "following own misdeed" was high in these cases.

Figures on any society that is sufficiently developed to have gathered statistics show the higher the standard of living the greater the proportion of older people. Scandinavia has an elderly segment possibly larger than ours (it was about 1% higher in the early 1960s), and the Common Market countries are, as a group, close to the U.S. The aging of all these societies is causing problems similar to our own. Family care is disappearing and institutional facilities for the elderly are being expanded in every developed country. Denmark is planning for residential and nursing-home accommodations for 4% of its older population. England and Wales, with over 2 1/2% of the elderly in institutional care, are expanding their facilities rapidly, especially those for women. Even in Italy, a society in which the extended family was long the norm, the old relationships are changing. A recent study of the age mix in a northern Italian industrial town of 80,000 found 13.4% of the populace over 65—and plans underway for expansion of institutions to care for them.

Our percentage of over-65's in the U.S. is moving up relentlessly from the 10% of a few years ago to the 15% of a few years hence. The other developed countries have a similar graph. (It is interesting to note that our planners once believed our over-65 population would stabilize at roughly 10%; a similar miscalculation in Europe visualized an 8.5% elderly population.) In the developing regions, meanwhile, the old people number only 3% to 4% of the population. This is comparable to our situation in 1900 when 4.1% of Americans were over 65. The United Nations statisticians estimated an over-65 world population of 200 million in the mid-1960s; they anticipate growth to 275 million by 1985 and to almost 400 million by the year 2000.

"Our society" is not an isolated, vicious persecutor of its old. We may wallow conspicuously in the guilt we seem to enjoy by accenting our shortcomings, but in any broad view we look fairly ordinary, a bit above average, and unlikely to regress in search of a Utopian myth.

9

LOOKING AHEAD

Looking ahead is scary business. A recent
book by researcher-on-aging Albert Rosenfeld is titled *Prolongevity*. This seems to be a newly coined
word for a predictable, if distressing, situation. We
are coping badly with longevity, but here comes *pro*
longevity with its threat of adding centuries instead
of mere years or decades to our life span. Figures
like 200 to 500 (additional) years now are bruited
about, often accompanied by the prediction that
sooner or later no one will die except by accident or
intent. We all know about accidents. But when will
death-by-intent become a ready and respectable option?

The *struldbruggs,* or immortals, of Swift's *Gulliver's
Travels* had not only "all the follies and infirmities
of other old men, but many more which arose from
the dreadful prospect of never dying." At least there
were relatively few *struldbruggs* and they were maintained, after eighty, as public charges or through
funds reserved for that purpose from their dis-

tributed estates. They did not deteriorate further after ninety but continued on in a static pattern, with the diseases they were subject to "neither increasing or diminishing."

Optimists predict that the diseases we are subject to will be conquered and that our "prolongevity" will, in time, be a healthy period. Possibly so—but there will be, *is,* an interim period during which our departure is delayed when too many of us remain in a holding-pattern of suffering and confusion.

Even assuming tremendously better health and tremendously more alert minds (neither of which can come quickly or cheaply), the next fifty to a hundred years look like rough going.

Money, for instance. Dr. Robert N. Butler, first director of the new National Institute on Aging (possibly better known as Pulitzer Prize winner for his book on aging, *Why Survive?*) told a meeting of the Gerontological Society that (as reported by the *New York Times,* October 19, 1976) "last year the elderly occupied one-third of all hospital beds for the acutely ill at a cost of $118.7 billion." These massive expenditures, which outdistance our notorious billions for defense, must come from our productive society. They will take a larger and larger slice. One cannot help wondering what portion of them goes to unquestionably terminal patients whose only wish is that they were not there.

122 More puzzling than the prospective source of

funds is the source of sufficient human caretakers to provide the services that are becoming accepted as minimal requirements for the elderly. Our 15,000 nursing homes have more than one-half as many fulltime helpers as they have residents (14,873 homes; 1,107,358 beds; 559, 684 fulltime personnel, according to the 1977 almanac). Doubling the number of institutions means doubling staff requirements. Efforts to avoid institutional care mean more and more parttime helpers, visiting nurses, dieticians, therapists, counselors, and so on. Such jobs, expecially at the lower levels, are not everyone's cup of tea. A half-hour visit to a nursing home—even a good one—can seem endless. An eight-hour shift of duty must be a real trial. Some attendants, one hears and believes, are fiends. Others—patient, kindly, rarely running out of affection—are veritable saints. And saints cannot be expected to multiply at the rate of the over-65 demand, nor to remain static and saintly through the years.

The problem of jobs *for* the old, as well as jobholders to look after them, looms as a sizable topic for the future. The whole question of how many people we will need in our changing society is up in the air. Some say the old will be better used because they will be absolutely necessary (the good news), while others predict shorter work days in a shortened work week for everyone, and more of the dust-heap, sooner, for the elderly.

Alvin Toffler, in *Future Shock,* brings up valid questions about our adjustment to added years. Can marriages, for example, be expected to last indefinitely? (Marriages between Swift's *struldbruggs* were automatically dissolved when the younger of the pair reached 80—"for the law thinks it a reasonable indulgence that those who are condemned without any fault of their own to a perpetual continuance in the world, should not have their misery doubled by the load of a wife.") Whether that reads "wife" or "husband," Swift had a point. And if serial marriages followed by "geriatric group marriages" (Mr. Toffler's term for the geriatric commune already coming into being on a small scale) become the trend, there will be increasingly less "family" concern for the individual aging grandparent whose grandparenthood is fractionally divided among half a dozen nonfamilies.

In any case, the continuity between generations is quickly disappearing. An earth message to a distant satellite is received with more understanding than many mother-to-daughter exchanges today. Siblings separated by only a few years now speak of a "generation gap" and college upperclassmen cite that gap in their reluctance to counsel freshmen. Too many years of life, juxtaposed with the changing landscape brought about by new technologies, can make us strangers in a strange land.

124   Science fiction often has provided clues for spe-

cific future prospects, but in the case of old-age suicide we draw mostly a blank. In Aldous Huxley's
Brave New World the only suicide is the Savage's
hanging. The old were not permitted to age in appearance ("We give them transfusions of young
blood. We keep their metabolism permanently
stimulated") but they died young in any case by our
standards: "Youth almost unimpaired till sixty, and
then, crack! the end." Death took place quickly in
Galloping Senility wards of special hospitals. (Interesting that the young Huxley apparently perceived
senility as a necessary prelude to death—he envi-
sioned it as being speeded up rather than elimi-
nated.)

Much speculation about the "conquering" of
aging is based on research involving the division and
multiplication—hence renewing—of body cells.
The number of times cells divide appears to govern
life span. Fifty is the significant number in humans
as against 25 divisions in chickens, who can live up
to 30 years, or 12 in mice, who have a three-year life
span. This cell division work is only one aspect of the
research on aging, but it is popular and was described a couple of years ago in large-circulation
magazines and in terms for the layman. In an article
in *Ladies' Home Journal,* Isaac Asimov pointed out an
important fact ignored in many of the articles: brain
cells are not involved in the dividing and renewal
process. We are born with all the brain cells we will 125

have; when they deteriorate they are not renewed.

This does not guarantee senility, and there are many approaches and many opinions—but it does make one think. Sir George Pickering, Regius professor of medicine at Oxford, has voiced a warning about the possibility that "those with senile brains will form an ever increasing fraction of the inhabitants of the earth." He finds this, obviously, a "terrifying prospect."

Dr. Robert N. Butler (quoted above) of *Why Survive?* notes in his comments on preventive medicine in that book that we spent in a specified year $410 per American citizen on defense, $19 on the space program and 89 cents on cancer research. And yet he also is quoted by the author of an article on nursing homes (Susan Jacoby in the *New York Times Magazine,* March 31, 1974) as saying: "It's absolutely terrifying—what happens when there is just one more big medical breakthrough—say, in the treatment of cancer? How many more people will be living beyond the point where they can take care of themselves?"

(Is 89 cents worth, then, *too* much cancer research?)

It is easy to see why most doctors have both ambivalent and terrified moments when they contemplate the future. They see the possible horrors and, as clearly, the inevitable need to go ahead. Research problems, like mountains, are there to be conquered

126

and they will be conquered. We cannot, and probably should not, argue about that. But we *can* argue our case for not being required to remain as slow-witted spectators of a process we do not comprehend.

An English friend, Millicent, who lived as a child with her colonial-service parents in one of the Rhodesias, recalls how she and her friends used to tease the elderly grandmother who shared their home. Perhaps "tease" is not the word, because the girls' relationship with the old lady was more accidental than deliberate. They discovered, while playing at "dress up" one afternoon on the verandah, that they had become, in their funny old hats and gowns, real-life characters out of the grandmother's past. Suddenly they had come to tea. She was so happy to see them. She rose to the occasion and ordered the servants to bring special treats. The servants, apparently understanding, joined in the game. Everyone was happy—most of all the grandmother. She recalled old times and bestowed unfamiliar names on her little guests. She chattered enough not to notice their inept response.

The tea party was repeated a few times when Millicent's mother was not at home. Then somehow the secret became known. Millicent was scolded and shamed. The trunk of dress-up clothes was locked away in the box room and Millicent was prohibited from having playmates at the house when her mother was out. The grandmother shed tears a couple of times because "they don't come to tea with me now—they've forgotten me."

Millicent, herself a grandmother, describes the memory with mixed feelings. "I remember Grandmother kindly, of course," she says, "but hardly as a real functioning person. And it's my *only* memory of her, unfortunately." She shivers. "I'd *hate* to have the kids remember me that way."

Today's children aren't likely to have such memories. The rather elaborate stage-set of verandahed house, tea on call and understanding household staff is as rare now as is the extended family. The grandparent who approaches senility today may be institutionalized or, if able to remain in a family setting, probably will be a responsibility, in part, of the young members. The summer "job" of 11-year-old Julie in a midwestern community was to keep an eye on her grandmother, confined to a wheelchair, when both parents were at work. It was a stop-gap plan they hoped could postpone the nursing home at least until fall. The mother returned at lunch time each day to help with the bathroom trip and to supervise feeding and medication, but Julie had sole responsibility for several hours at a time.

The old lady liked to be wheeled out onto a low porch where she seemed to enjoy watching birds. One afternoon, when Julie had been given the added task of being sure to take phone messages because her salesman father was expecting a specific call, the phone rang at just the wrong moment. She didn't take time to check the brake on the chair, which she had just moved out of the too-strong sun, and when she got back she found her grandmother off the porch, half-tipped into a geranium bed, muttering unpleasantly. A neighbor came, a doctor was called. No new breaks. All was well.

But later the grandmother complained to her daughter. "Who *is* that little girl who keeps pestering me?" she asked. "She pushed me off the porch —that's no way to treat an old lady. You should tell her to go away."

In this case the tears were Julie's, who had to be told because responsibility for a senile person requires knowing the score.

Some of our senility today probably is a pseudosenility induced by drugs. To make the anxious elderly person more tractable, many doctors prescribe rather too liberally. Sometimes this allows a person to put off the day of institutional living, or it may quiet unreasonable fears of a temporary nature. But too much "tranquillizing" over a long period of time can turn us into the familiar "zombies" who pace with a staring-eyed restlessness through nursing home corridors.

We have a right to keep all the wits we have about us. It is a fiction that old age is a time of serenity— and the false serenity of the drugged is the last thing   129 we need. We must hang on to our hostility, un-masked, so long as we are capable of control—it may help us recognize the approach of actual senility and make our plans.

This bad-news chapter ends with one bright bit of research. The writer of the Suicide coverage for the new *Encyclopaedia Britannica* reassures us about "Suicide in the Future": " . . . It is difficult to imagine man in the future without this potential, which has sometimes been proclaimed as one of the basic human freedoms. Suicidal acts will continue to be committed. There are no prospects that an anti-suicidal substance will be discovered in the foreseeable future."

10

ME . . . AND US

Our era is, according to the popular press, a time of accent on *Me*. Bugged perhaps by being too frequently a mere computer number, today's individual shouts out her or his identity and rights.

Even the old—our fastest-growing minority—have the right to say *Me too*. We have no obligation to abandon our preferences and opinions just because our weakening voices may be outshouted.

The decision we may make in choosing suicide is *ours* to make. It is our life we are giving up, our death we are arranging. The choice does not infringe on the rights of others. We do not need to explain and excuse.

Daniel C. Maguire, a theology professor whose *Death by Choice* examines in some depth the moral aspects of euthanasia, accents that "Many people have difficulty believing that they have moral authority over their dying. One of the principal reasons why this question is opening up for reconsideration today is that the idea of authority is being rethought."

The rethinking contributes to the "me" attitude. It gives us autonomy if we have the courage to take it and use it. Psychiatry professor Thomas Szasz, in his *Ceremonial Chemistry,* says on the subject: "Autonomy is the death knell of authority, and authority knows it: hence the ceaseless warfare of authority against the exercise, both real and symbolic, of autonomy—that is, against suicide, against masturbation, against self-medication, against the proper use of language itself!"

We give up our autonomy too easily when we become old and weak. Many who wish to die will live on because of their family's pride, their doctor's principles, their formal affiliation with a church, or a community attitude that sees suicide as a blot on the record. The choice will be made by "them." The suffering will be for "me."

It need not be so.

The voice of "us" is of course stronger than of a single "me." We who are growing old are not used to the mutual-support concepts of the "sisterhood," but we should be capable of learning them in a good cause. We are very much in this prolongevity pickle together—the young and the old. Each must be the caretaker and the cared-for through the extended years with which we are threatened.

We all have a stake in gaining the right to say no to life at a time of our choosing. We want to make it legal. Pending legality, we can use as many innovative ways as possible to keep old-age suicide a lively topic, openly discussed.

All of us can contribute by making no effort to cover up or disguise a known suicide. The braver among us, who might "aid and abet" secretly but not openly, can change our ways and talk about it. We can lend support—in words or funds or whatever is needed—in cases that might come to litigation. (Such cases are needed, actually, to get a few legal precedents and provide enough publicity to back up efforts for reform.)

We can take polls, and publicize the results, on all aspects of euthanasia and suicide. If anyone has polled the aging on these subjects, the results have not been published widely enough to be located in routine research, even though legislators who have introduced euthanasia bills report a good volume of favorable response from the elderly. Younger pollers probably have difficulty asking straight-out questions about suicide when they are dealing with their seniors. We are not inhibited by this factor and it's time to know something about how our over-65's really express themselves (when given a chance) on the subject.

We can reassure the timid that we are working only for a right of choice—not trying to eliminate the old—and that a right to live is inherent in a right to die.

We can supply, as a group, a depository for witnessed letters of intent, periodically renewed, until such time as there may be a legal means for prerecording the intention to accomplish suicide. As caretakers of such letters of intent, we can be sure that they are made known to the proper persons if or when their authors become incapable of decisions. We can offer guidance on what we believe that author's wish would be, on the basis of continuity through (to borrow an accountant's phrase) "accepted principles consistently applied."

We can work cooperatively with euthanasia organizations and can collect signatures for petitions backing relevant legislation. We can try to broaden any proposed euthanasia legislation to include (if it does not do so) provision for aid-to-suicide (but we should not make this effort if it will impede the passage of a law that is useful even though it falls short of our aim).

Most of all, we can give *group* support to encourage ourselves and each other. If the suicide of an elderly woman were followed by a dignified announcement that her death was a planned death with the help of friends who also planned, in time, to go the same way—this, for a while at least, would be news. By the time such instances cease to be news, we all will have a legally protected right to opt out.

134

I have a fantasy in which a small crowd of us, wearing summer pastels and prints, wide-brimmed hats and white or beige arch-support shoes, makes a chattering departure from a boat rental pier on a quiet lake. Browned young men, polite and friendly, help us aboard. Then we are on our own, in a landscape rich with the deep green technicolor shadings of a French film that specializes in lush countryside. We are in the midst of this green bounty, moving on our peaceful lake. We all are a little overweight perhaps. And in our amateur attempts at rowing, our much-given, little-accepted exchanges of advice, our inattention to the task—somehow we become alarmingly unsteady. But it is not alarming. It is funny, joyous. We shake with laughter and the boat shakes with us. Our overturning is rather gentle. Our laughter mingles with the splish-splosh of the disturbed water. Soon quiet returns. An overturned boat drifts among floating hats. On a peaceful, beautiful day.

"Drowning is too back-to-the-womb," a friend tells me. "And I doubt if it's that easy for anyone who swims halfway well."

She will swim well at ninety, I suspect, and her fantasy is pure frontier. "Maybe he's death, the great lover," she says. "Anyway, he carries two guns and we have our rendevous in a saloon-like bar. But luxurious—you know? Ripe leather and polished wood. He buys me a neat whisky and we talk about 135 his beautiful guns. They *are* beautiful. Lots of intricate design in the metal. And heavy. I lift one. He speaks of Russian Roulette. I believe there are no empty chambers in this heavy gun. And then there is a sound of firing. I notice the men at the bar turn their heads toward our table. Slowly, like a replayed sport detail. And—well, that's all."

"The man—gun-toting Death or whoever. Is he young or old?"

"Funny," she says. "I never noticed."

"But who needs a fantasy?" someone else asks. "I push on to the other side of the gap. I really believe there could be something to this life-mass concept. But if I return as a tree I don't want it to be a long-life redwood. Something brief and blooming and spectacular—"

"And *that's* not a fantasy?" The interruption, with laughter, changes the subject.

But it will change back, on this day or another. Because common-sense suicide is a good topic. Let's start talking about it.

A PERSONAL WORD

Most of the books and articles on suicide are, and no doubt should be, written by experts of one kind or another. The authors may be psychologists or sociologists, MD's, psychiatrists, anthropologists, or specialists in social history. I have only one qualification for the task: I am a woman in the age group that is the subject of this study. Some of my friends approved of the effort, others did not. One of the less polite said, "Why do you want to dig around in all that morbid research? Why don't you write about something cheerful?"

What could be more cheerful than avoiding a distasteful death of the common hospital or nursing-home variety? Nevertheless, his words gave me something to think about. What *do* I expect to get out of it?

Well, for one thing I have already achieved a comfortable "at home" feeling with the vocabulary and general idea of suicide. And my vague ideas of how-to are more concrete and practical after looking into methodology. I will avoid the worst mistakes. These are measurable benefits already recognized. Financial benefit? Probably not. The average book advance for an unknown writer might pay for a month in a so-so urban nursing home, or even two or three months in the hinterlands.

But if the book is well received by the readers toward whom it is directed, a big plus is to come: enough response to allow the formation of Happy Hemlock Mutual Aid Cell Number One (or whatever more sensible name is chosen) and my own quiet incorporation into it.

It will be a big relief.

SOURCE READING

Alvarez, Alfred. *The Savage God.* New York: Random House, 1972.

Bruller, Jean. *21 Delightful Ways to Commit Suicide.* New York: Covici, 1930.

Bunzel, Bessie (see Dublin, Louis I.)

Butler, Robert N. *Why Survive?* New York: Harper & Row, 1975.

Cavan, Ruth. *Suicide.* New York: Russel & Russel, 1965 (University of Chicago Sociological Series). First published in 1928.

Choron, Jacques. *Suicide.* New York: Charles Scribner's Sons, 1972.

de Beauvoir, Simone. *Coming of Age,* trans. by Patrick O'Brian. New York: Putnam, 1972.

Donne, John. *Biathanatos.* New York: The Facsimile Text Society 1930 (reproduced from the first edition.

Downing, A. B., ed. *Euthanasia and the Right to Death: The Case for Voluntary Euthanasia.* London: Peter Owen, 1969.

Dublin, Louis I. and Bessie Bunzel. *To Be Or Not To Be.* New York: Harrison Smith and Robert Haas, 1933.

Dublin, Louis I. *Suicide.* New York: Ronald Press, 1963.

Durkheim, Emile. *Suicide,* trans. by John A. Spaulding

and George Simpson. New York: The Free Press, 1951.

Encyclopaedia Britannica, 15th ed. 1974. *"Suicide."* Macropaedia, Vol. 17.

Encyclopedia of Religion and Ethics. New York: Charles Scribner's Sons, 1951.

Eusebius Pamphili. *The Ecclesiastical History,* trans. by Kirsopp Lake, D.D., D.Litt. London: Heinemann, 1926.

Farber, Maurice L. *Theory of Suicide.* New York: Funk & Wagnalls, 1968.

Farberow, Norman L. *Taboo Topics.* New York: Atherton Press, 1963. (See also Shneidman, Edwin S.)

Gibbs, Jack P. *Suicide.* New York: Harper & Row (Readers in Social Problems series), 1968.

Heifetz, Milton D. with Charles Mangel. *The Right to Die.* New York: G. P. Putnam's Sons, Berkley Medallion Book, 1975.

Hendin, Herbert. *Suicide and Scandinavia.* New York: Grune & Stratton, 1964.

Hume, David. "On Suicide" in *Essays, Moral, Political and Literary.* New York: Oxford Press, 1963.

Huxley, Aldous. *Brave New World.* New York: Harper & Row (Perennial Classic ed.), 1969.

Litman, Robert E. (see Shneidman, Edwin S.)

Maguire, Daniel C. *Death by Choice.* New York: Schocken Books, 1975.

Mangel, Charles (see Heifetz, Milton D.)

Mannes, Marya. *Last Rights.* New York: New American Library, 1973.

Masaryk, Thomas G. *Suicide and the Meaning of Civilization,* trans. by William B. Weist and Robert G. Batson. Chicago and London: University of Chicago Press, 1970.

Meaker, Marijane. *Sudden Endings.* New York: Double-
day, 1964.

Meerloo, Joost A. M. *Suicide and Mass Suicide.* New York:
Grune & Stratton, 1962.

Mendelson, Mary Adelaide. *Tender Loving Greed.* New
York: Knopf, 1974.

Menninger, Karl. *Man Against Himself.* New York: Harcourt Brace Jovanovich, 1938.

Metropolitan Life Insurance Company. *Statistical Bulletin.*
New York, May, 1976.

Montaigne, Michel Eyquem de. *Essays,* trans. by Donald
M. Frame. Stanford, Calif.: Stanford University Press,
1958.

Montesquieu, Baron de. *Persian Letters,* trans. by J. Robert Loy. New York: Meridian Books, 1961.

Perlin, Seymour, ed. *A Handbook for the Study of Suicide,*
New York: Oxford University Press, 1975.

Russell, O. Ruth, *Freedom to Die,* New York: Dell,
1976.

Shneidman, Edwin S. and Norman L. Farberow (eds.),
Clues to Suicide, New York: McGraw-Hill, 1957.

Shneidman, Edwin S., N. L. Farberow, and Robert E.
Litman. *The Psychology of Suicide.* New York: Science
House, 1970.

Simmons, Leo W. *The Role of the Aged in Primitive Society.*
Hamdon, Conn.: Archon Books, 1970.

Stengel, Erwin. *Suicide and Attempted Suicide.* Baltimore:
Penguin Books, 1964.

Swift, Jonathan. *Gulliver's Travels and Other Writings,* ed-
ited by Louis A. Landa. Boston: Houghton Mifflin Co.,
1960.

Szasz, Thomas. *Ceremonial Chemistry.* Garden City, N.Y.:
Anchor Press, 1974.

Toffler, Alvin. *Future Shock.* New York: Random House, 1970.

Wertenbaker, Lael (Tucker). *Death of a Man.* Boston: Beacon Press, 1974.

West, Jessamyn. *The Woman Said Yes.* New York: Harcourt Brace Jovanovich, 1976.

Williams, Glanville. *The Sanctity of Life and the Criminal Law.* New York: Knopf, 1957.

World Health Organization. *Prevention of Suicide.* Public Health Papers No. 35, Geneva, 1968.

World Health Organization. *Suicide and Attempted Suicide.* Public Health Papers No. 58, Geneva, 1974.

Other books from The Hemlock Society

(A non-profit educational corporation supporting the option of active voluntary
euthanasia for the terminally ill.)

Let Me Die Before I Wake
By Derek Humphry

Discussion and guidance on the problems associated with dignified
self-deliverance. Outlines methods of rational suicide.

$10.   Distributed by Grove Press
                                                      New York

Jean's Way
By Derek Humphry with Ann Wickett

The true story of one woman's plans to end her own life towards
the end of a terminal illness. This book is helpful to other couples
in a similar predicament.

$8   Distributed by Grove Press
                                                      New York

Assisted Suicide: The Compassionate Crime

A compilation of famous euthanasia cases from around the world.
Invaluable as source material for researchers.

$5 (includes mailing)   Only from The Hemlock Society

Who Believes in Voluntary Euthanasia?

A survey of Hemlock's membership in 1982. Important research
data.

$4. (includes mailing)   Only from The Hemlock Society.
                                            P.O. Box 66218
                                            Los Angeles, CA 90066

THE HEMLOCK SOCIETY

Founded 1980 in Los Angeles
Supports the option of active voluntary euthanasia
for the terminally ill and the seriously incurably ill mature adult.

• •

If you are in agreement with the general philosophy expressed in "Commonsense Suicide: The Final Right" you may wish to join the Hemlock Society. (Membership costs $15 a year.)

1. By joining you are helping to convince those around you that you are sincere in your belief in this concept.

2. You receive a quarterly newsletter which keeps you up to date with national and international developments in euthanasia.

3. Your support helps the Hemlock Society in its educative efforts and its long-range plan to reform the law on euthanasia.

The Hemlock Society
A non-profit educational group
IRS tax code 501c3

Mailing address:

PO Box 66218
Los Angeles
CA 90066

Telephone: (213) 391-1871